S0-BNX-978

Praise for

Dragon Spirit:
How to Self-Market Your Dream

"Why are we surprised to discover that the success of a business has more to do with what we bring to it than what's in the business plan? This delicious book will improve your attitude, streamline your life, and radically improve your chances for success."   —Seth Godin, columnist *Fast Company*, author of *Unleashing the Ideavirus, Survival Is Not Enough* and *Purple Cow*

"Ride the Dragon if you want to be successful beyond your wildest dreams."   —Al and Laura Ries, authors of *The Fall of Advertising and the Rise of PR*

"Once again, a book written by the original Zentrepreneurs has crossed my desk. I was changed for the better after reading their first volume. And after reading their latest work, I am nothing except positive that my dreams can become real. I've taken the time to savor this book. It's street-wise, business-world savvy and just plain life-enhancing. Simply put—this book is wonderful. I've made it mandatory re-reading."   —Reader from Detroit, MI

Praise for

Success at Life:
How to Catch and Live Your Dream

"This is a book filled with grace and beauty and desire. I can offer no higher accolade. Business as passion. Business as cause. Read. Ponder. Act. Contribute. Passionately. Please!"
          —Tom Peters, author of *Re-imagine!* and *The Brand You 50*

"My kind of book—short, sweet, and to the point. The writing is snappy and fresh, the advice dead-on."   —Cheryl Richardson, author of *Stand Up for Your Life*

"*Success at Life* is a motivational journey of enlightenment and re-discovery charged with humor, encouragement, and entrepreneurial wisdom. Don't start a new career without reading this book."
          —Jeffrey J. Fox, author of *How to Make Big Money in Your Own Small Business*

Other Books by Ron Rubin and Stuart Avery Gold:

Success at Life: How to Catch and Live Your Dream

Tea Chings: The Tea and Herb Companion

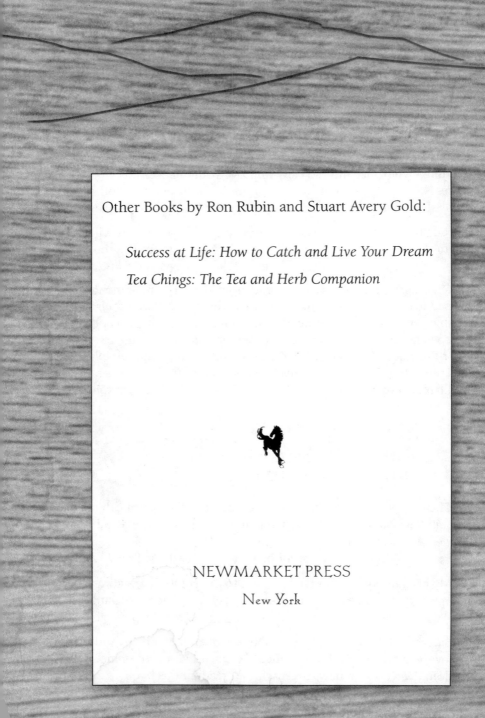

NEWMARKET PRESS

New York

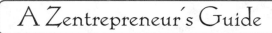

A Zentrepreneur's Guide

dragon spirit

How to Self-Market Your Dream

RON RUBIN AND STUART AVERY GOLD

MINISTERS OF The REPUBLIC of TEA

Copyright © 2003 by Ron Rubin and Stuart Avery Gold

This book is published in the United States of America. All rights reserved. This book may not be reproduced, in whole or in part, in any form, without written permission. Inquiries should be addressed to Permissions Department, Newmarket Press, 18 East 48th Street, New York, NY 10017.

Interior graphics by Image Studio Ltd.

1-55704-620-4 (paperback)
1-55704-563-1 (hardcover)

10   9   8   7   6   5   4   3   2   1

Calligraphy by Machiko

Library of Congress Cataloging-in-Publication Data

Rubin, Ron.
    Dragon spirit : how to self-market your dream / Ron Rubin and Stuart Avery Gold. —1st ed.
        p. cm.
    ISBN 1-55704-563-1 (Cloth : alk. paper)
    1. Marketing. I. Gold, Stuart Avery. II. Title.
HF5415.R83 2003
658.8—dc21

                                                        2003005446

QUANTITY PURCHASES

Companies, professional groups, clubs, and other organizations may qualify for special terms when ordering quantities of this title. For information, write Special Sales, Newmarket Press, 18 East 48th Street, New York, NY 10017, call (212) 832-3575, fax (212) 832-3629, or e-mail mail@newmarketpress.com

www.newmarketpress.com

Manufactured in the United States of America.
At the authors' request, this book has been printed on acid-free paper.

For Zentrepreneurs everywhere,

in hopes that a word or two endures

to mingle with your dreams.

~•~

"If you ignore the dragon, it will eat you.

If you try to confront the dragon, it will overpower you.

If you ride the dragon, you will take advantage of

its might and power."

—Chinese proverb

Contents

做夢

ZUOMENG
Dream

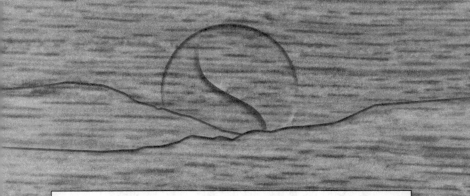

Chapter One
THE DREAM

WARMING THE KETTLE,
STEEPING THE DREAM

Change is a dragon—ride it and transform.

This book took 5,000 years to write.

Give or take a few weeks, beginning with a jagged line of history dating back to 2737 B.C., when on a Tuesday morning the Chinese Emperor Shen Nong discovered that tea leaves infused in hot water and slowly sipped were, well, something wondrous. Heads cleared, spirits soared, and thoughts focused. From there, wind the clock to show a few more emperors. Add to that a bunch more dynasties. Toss into the mix the growth of Buddhism and Taoism, some Portuguese explorers, England's Queen Catherine, some new world taxes, a tea party in Boston harbor, and then fast forward to 1992 to a powerful exhilarating dream to create a tea revolution, and here we are.

The Republic of Tea: a progressive, socially conscious California company whose history and philosophy have magically come to life for readers as the subject of two already bestselling books and via countless media articles. But nevertheless, since we will be referencing The Republic in much of what is to come, we would like to take a stuttering step here to let the reader know one or two of the huzzahs already documented in those printed pages, the first of which is this:

It's not totally the tea.

Well, it is and it isn't.

Truth to tell, The Republic of Tea sells not only the most exquisite teas and herbs in the whole wide world, it also offers as part of its award-winning line, all kinds of good stuff: healthy chai tea lattes, bottled varietal iced teas, tea jams, tea honey, teacups, and teapots, plus a dizzying array of other tea-related products that you can nail down by way of our catalogue, Website, and in more than 20,000 gourmet and specialty food retailers, restaurants, and cafés throughout the country. But like we said, truth to tell, it's not totally the tea—

Not entirely.

Shhhhh . . . It's also the dream.

The dream to create a Tea Revolution, by infusing our culture with a new and relevant tea ceremony, one which draws on the awesome, rich history of tea, recent scientific discoveries, and the growing trends for a healthier, happier, and more attentive life. Can you imagine a dream more tangible and sanguine?

No matter. The idea had found us. And dream-weavers we had become.

Harnessing all our creativity, skills, knowledge, and a passion for the possible, we have blissfully brought the seductive boundlessness of our dream to fruition. A dream to present a new way of marketing the world's oldest commodity and, in so doing, offer a fresh and welcome philosophy that becomes a reflective catalyst for positive, fundamental change for all who journey to our fanciful land.

And journey they do, immigrating to the sip-by-sip life—a life of health, balance, and well-being. Where with each visit, a sip of fragrant, full-leaf, steamy tea allows customers to bring back and incorporate into their daily lives a path to wholeness and longevity. The Republic of Tea is a vehicle that engages us to get in touch with the beauty and the wonder of our lives, and delivers us through a journey of many cups to a product and a message that transcends, by capturing the imagination and inspiring one and all to travel toward a more peaceful and fulfilling lifestyle.

By taking the time for tea, we create an exquisite encounter for ourselves. Slowing down to take life sip by sip, rather than gulp by gulp, we perceive a clarity of purpose and an exuberance for the gift of life that we have been given. By selling tea we are indirectly selling awareness. Of course, the absolute truth is that we are only the merchants of awareness; it's the tea that sells the TeaMind and expands your world into a new-lived reality, if you will only open yourself to the awareness it tries to deliver.

Through enthusiastically living a dream defined, we have come to realize that a dream is not an it, it is an us, our spiritual signature, a life-force that is greater than ourselves that works itself through us, awakening the soul, rhythming the heart, and allowing for the changing and growing self.

The point being that for Ron and me, The Republic of Tea is, yes, a bubble of a dream come true, but more than that it is a business, but very much more than that, it is, above all else, an experience. A meaningful experience that millions and more a day are wanting to share. That is the key to its place in the world. While a product meets a need, an experience fulfills a desire. Yours, mine, theirs. And since much of what follows in this book is an invitation to walk out into the light, know that at the heart of the dream that has become The Republic of Tea is a marketing wake-up call that should be the pulse of whatever dream business that embodies your own soul and wishes to succeed and it is crucial: In building your business, a customer is not someone who buys your idea, product, or service . . . a customer is someone who becomes part of it.

Pssst . . . remember that last sentence, because in marketing your dream this is one of the thunder claps in heaven you must pay attention to.

Followed hard by this:

In business, any business that you start, it is you who must assume the responsibility to make it thrive. The mantra of any business is to be successful. And if a business is to be successful it must face up to absolute economic realities, the primary of which is that it must make a profit. And in order for profit to increase, for business to survive and flourish, it is paramount that a mindfulness be paid to the needs and wants of the customer—a first and foremost focus on customers that engages them in a personal dialogue that connects them to your product or service in a profound way.

That being stated, know that the only true way to achieve this is by rising above the hollowness of mass marketing, abandoning the entanglements of seller, transcending to become the customer. By relinquishing the opiates of marketing, and letting go of the language of the seller, you will approach business from the needs of the customer, not yours. And if you will not accept this, we will not weep for you as you go down. While America's largest companies fiddle in panic spending kajillions in trying to establish the psychological marketing strategy that Madison Avenue defines as emotional branding, we of The Republic of Tea openly embody the words of Lao-Tzu who said, "The way to do is to be."

As Zentrepreneurs, we are guided by the ageless and timeless wind of wisdom that whispers to us the splendid ancient teaching of the world's oldest book, the Chinese classic *I Ching*, "Look at someone else as you would yourself." How simple. By projecting ourselves outward we travel inward, reaching the ultimate reality of letting in what is in the hearts and minds of others. Setting aside the inexorable goal of market share, we invite the organic process of mind share and, in so doing, reach the collective consciousness where the Zentrepreneur's philosophy of life embodies the Zentrepreneur's philosophy of business.

And is this so important?

Very.

Perhaps the most important, one true thing you must run with when you set this primer down—the happy ending, which is of such lasting import, we are compelled to break writing rule of thumb number one by giving it to you here, right out of the chute, in the first pages, rather than in the last, so you can have it quickly, all fresh and spanking shiny, before we gear up and get started.

Ready?

Realize, please:

While entrepreneurs get hold of an idea, Zentrepreneurs allow an idea to get hold of them.

There. The great bracing truth we want to wallpaper you with. And if you will commit this simple touchstone to memory and arm yourself with it above all else in your arsenal, the gods will smile down.

Forever.

Know that it isn't the mind that possesses an idea, but it is the idea that possesses the mind. Once an idea gets hold of you, it inhabits you and takes over your dreams and desires. Pulled by its powerful potential, it will sweep you off your feet, permeate your being, electrify, excite, and inspire—it will dramatically change your needs and your wants. Floating free of any mental gravity, you will find yourself driven by no other motive than the experiencing of your own freedom and happiness that comes from living the life you dream of.

Great wonders will demand to fall into place.

Nothing more clearly indicates what the core of this book will openly offer: a practical philosophy to overcome the challenges of creating a business, by embracing new ways of seeing, thinking, feeling, and doing. You will be encouraged to stretch yourself beyond the reach of ordinary awareness, to unleash your full potential, to identify your work purpose, and to empower your unique talents, your special gifts, and accomplished skills. As Zentrepreneurs we are all *long de chuan ren*, Chinese for "descendants of the spiritual dragon"—symbols of sense, spirit, creativity, vitality, and will. Zentrepreneurs, like the dragon, wield the power of countless changes and transformations. And as readers of our previous excursion, *Success at Life: How to Catch and Live Your Dream*, hopefully took to heart, life is an ongoing dialogue with change. And change for Zentrepreneurs, like the beauty of a flower, is ordinary activity. This still is and always will be true.

Understand something: By possessing the glorious power of change, Zentrepreneurs recognize that they are one with their dream, their nature—their imaginative and spiritual strength. When they follow their nature, they follow their *Te*, or natural way—their soul, their talents, their gifts, their passion, their power, their deep sense of who they are and how they wish to be.

Zentrepreneurs are guided by their heart and flow in

complete accord with the path they must follow, leading to the life they were born to live. When you are in complete accord with the design of your true path, it is possible to respond to change naturally, without resistance or hesitation. Following the path of least resistance is the result of traveling your chosen path with direction, self-esteem, confidence, discipline, and enthusiasm— soaring the dragon—which will deliver you to the success of your dreams with ease. The Chinese ancients believed that if you breathe life and energy into your spiritual dragon, or your greater self, you create change that breathes life and energy into all, allowing you to ride the dragon's expansive spirit to a zenith of endless possibilities.

Your dream.

Your destiny.

We tell you this because there is a lesson here. Actually, two. The first of which is this: In business, as in life, we all need all the good advice we can get. And the second: Good advice is always there for us, if we are simply there for it.

An example: As Ministers of The Republic of Tea, several times a year, Ron and I turn days upside down, trekking to the misty green hills of famed tea provinces, searching for and sampling rare exquisite teas. These prized teas are the product of expert cultivation and perfect timing, with varied and unique characteristics similar to those of truly interesting wines. So extraordinary are these finds, so exciting their discovery, because they are not mass-grown but nurtured on single estates often by a single family.

It was on one such journey through China's Fujian province that a bamboo raft took us through the canyons and many windings of *Jiuqu Xi*, or Nine Bend Creek—an awesome experience. Truly it was. The perfect beauty and the silence of the scenery were breathtaking, and, believe me, soon so were we, as we were many hours later huffing and puffing our way up the precipices and peaks of the legendary Wuyi Mountains in quest of the rare Yancha, or "cliff tea," sometimes referred to as "monkey-picked tea." Now they call it monkey tea because it is said that only the most agile simians are employed to perform the difficult doing of plucking the tender shoots from the dizzying heights at which it is grown. I don't know whether the monkey-picked business is myth or legend and, then again, I don't know a whole lot of things. But one thing I do know and that is, to this day, I don't think I've ever been more wide-eyed and very much concentrated on my footing as when Ron and I went about making our way to that mountaintop. And then, finally, blessedly, triumphantly, we completed our climb, and moments later we were on our way to the sublime splendor of our glorious destination.

Shangri-la.

And if you had been tagging along when we got to where we were going, guess what—you would have thought that you had been part of some cruel trick.

Whipped. Standing on the tippy-toes of your Timberlands, squinting with bewilderment at the madness of the moment, you would have wondered about this climaxing of our pilgrimage and asked, Do we have the right address—did we screw up? But in this part of the world there are no addresses. And for good reason: Who needs an address to hang your hat on when your mud-bricked home has been in the same place for more than 500 years? That's how far back the house had been the residence for generations of the Lee family and you have to understand, what's 500 years—nothing—when the area just celebrated its 2,200th anniversary, rivaling the history of Alexandria in Egypt and Rome in Italy. If you were to say that this was just a small dirt-trodden structure, we would agree with you. If you were to say that this sure took some tough travel to get here, we would agree with you all the way. And if we were to say that the absolute awe of the panoramic view that the house commanded made one heck of a case for beauty unmatched anywhere on our globe, you would agree with us all the way.

And do not doubt our excitement as our guide trooped Ron and me up the trail to the humble, simple, thatched hut, because we had a hot lead that here was where we were to find the family that had been the earthly source for the heavenly fabled and cherished Yancha tea.

The Lees were not a young group—time had etched them all. The deepest grooves were on Mr. Lee, who was remarkably into his eighties and not even he could tell you how much into them he was. Mrs. Lee was younger then her husband, but not by too many years. And their son, already leathery and missing many teeth, obviously had the same family genes, and I would have to say he was somewhere occupying his stretch of sixties. Small in height, wispy in frame, but with wonderful weather-beaten faces full of character and all the smiles a mouthful of molars will allow, the Lees were a beautiful people. Clearly they had a little less then nothing, but looking at the shine in their eyes you knew that you were sharing space with truly contented beings. There is a Chinese proverb: "A heart at peace gives life to the body." The magical truth of that proverb endures with the harmony and tranquility exhibited by the Lee family.

Bowing hello, hello, loads of good will as the introductions were respectfully made.

The State Department should do so well.

Looking around, we assumed all of the workers were out working. We were wrong. They were all of the workers. For the Lees, every one of their waking hours were spent using their craft and all their indomitable skill toiling on the care and cultivation of the divine and magnificent *Camellia sinensis* bush. Tea was their work, their staff of life, and like their ancestors, they too were very much imbued with its spirit.

Now Mr. Lee was from the mountain, but his voice was from the sky. It was high and soft like a cloud, and even if you understood the dialect you would still have to strain an ear to hear, as he invited us in for the peace of mind and communion of soul that comes with the sharing in a bowl of tea.

While the Japanese in a formal ritual take time for the inner profoundness represented in the ceremony of preparing and serving tea to their guests, the Chinese simply take time for the tea, knowing that at the center of every human being is the spiritual taste of tea. Holding a bowl of tea in your hands, sipping its natural serenity, you can taste the solitude of nature. Soon the tea inhabits you and you the tea, and surrendering yourself to what has entered you, you reach an ineffable buoyancy of being, becoming one with all things, gaining an illumination that allows you to experience the fabric of life, nothing less than the very breathing of the earth itself.

The best of many good praises that can be sung for tea is that it creates TeaMind.

TeaMind is the mastery of mysteries—no hand can paint it, no voice can describe it. It is a stillness within activity, and activity within stillness—the wellspring of all possibilities, where good questions and smart ideas wait to be born. A natural state, it can ultimately be comprehended only through the experience of sipping the right tea. Sipping the grandiose gift of the leaf with Mr. Lee, TeaMind came about very quickly. And so too the good questions.

He started off by asking with great humility about our business and then with greater interest about our families and from there another question led to something else and then he was on a roll, the spontaneous questions buzzing our ears about this and about that, and he especially wanted to know stuff about America and that he once saw a photograph of New York and what can it be like to live in such place, and anytime you are peppered by one after another question from such an old and inquisitive but alert mind it is a good feeling. And believe it, peppered being a good choice of words you see, because sure Mr. Lee was old, and absolutely his voice was whisper weak, but let me tell you this, his mind was still sharp because with his questions came a mingling of opinions and brilliance that knocked us out. It didn't matter that his backed ached or that his neck hurt or that his legs numbed, he kept asking the questions—not a single rest if there was still something he wanted to know.

Until he raised his bony finger.

And apologized—

For asking so many questions. He asked did we mind and, of course, we said we didn't. Who could mind when you were in the presence of a wise one practiced in the art of knowing? And though we thought he was certainly sage, we were unquestionably convinced of that when he spoke in a voice lower and slower, the very line that still echoes in my head:

"Only the clamor for knowledge leads to the wisdom of humility."

And when I remember Mr. Lee, as often I do, I remember the power of those words, still clinging to their truth. The impelling logic of it all: That only those who know they know not can become wise. His advice offers, as your spiritual dragon does, a flight of transcendence and self-expansion, allowing you an upward and spiraling journey to create a dream that embodies the power, the passion, and the bounteous gifts that you can and must deliver to the world. Recognize that work and life are an interconnected adventure, guided by the heart, winged with spirit, and nourished by the soul. Circling back now, that is what a Zentrepreneur is, someone who endeavors to live a life in which what he or she does is one with what he or she is.

And so as Ron and I continue transversing our own odyssey of unmoored possibilities and growth, we urge you to use this paged companion as your passport to fulfillment, a guidebook for transformation outward and inward that will help you with discovering the secrets to marketing your dream. As travel-tried Zentrepreneurs we have set up sign posts, chartered from ancient wisdom and timeless philosophies, knotted together with state-of-the-art insights and observations that we have gleaned and embraced from our own collective years of experience and the experience of others. You will enjoy a pilgrimage down a path of clarity and calm that will demystify the joys and terrors of marketing a dream that captures your soul and addresses the realities of the marketplace.

We are confident that these pages will help you stay

the course and avoid the swirling mist-shrouded doubts and dilemmas, the obstacles of confusion and discontent, the always-waiting-around-every-corner, total panic that is also part of the path to success. We humbly offer these traveler's tales to encourage and inspire, inspirit and enthuse, or simply as a profundity of advice for the inner journey we all must travel in pursuit of our life's work. Know that every time someone finds his or her own way, he or she paves the way for others. That being said, here is as good a place as any for us to wedge in our plea—Remember again, please, with lasting import: Good advice is always there for us, if we are simply there for it.

We hope there's some here for you.

—*Stuart Avery Gold*

REQING

Passion

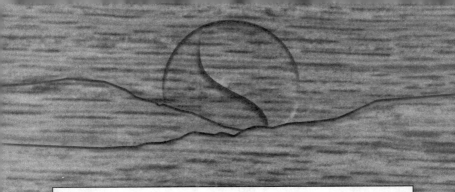

Chapter Two
PASSION

PAINT YOUR PASSION—
WHAT COLOR ARE HUE?

Everything great and colorful is

because of the dragon.

"It's the MTV!"

That's my mother talking. And as we begin to pound out pages for this, I take a few secs to go hiking back through the years and suddenly there she is, sitting on the sofa, close to the action, in front of the set.

"It's the MTV and all the Nintendo."

Invariably quick with an opinion whether solicited or not, my in-all-ways splendid mother was chatting it up, making it clear to Dan Rather, who of course wasn't anywhere within earshot. He was there on the tube, doing a story about the increasingly shorter attention span of the national populace. And you know what? Today, looking back on it, turns out that this particular pearl of my mother's wisdom was only true then and truer now.

Recent studies have found that an entire generation of Americans have been shaped by several societal and cultural factors—a blinding blizzard of fast-paced media, faster-placed sound bites, short snippets of image-grabbing MTV, spectacular video software, lightning hard drives, wondrous CD-ROMs, cable modem this and wireless that, the quicksilver of it all. Anybody who is reading this, whether you have taken the time to think of it or not, your noodles have certainly been shaped by this new center of unprecedented technology that hovers over our culture. While we have transformed the world with these technologies, do not make the mistake of losing sight of how these technologies have transformed us.

Everything is fast. The world is changing at light speed. People are shaving time off every task because fast and faster is no longer enough. Forget that at your peril. Unfortunately pencil-tapping impatience rules.

Meaning?

Only this: Time is precious. Zero people on the planet are interested in whatever babble it is that you think they need to hear or see. They would rather live their average days in a world where they didn't have to meet with you. And on the teenie-weenie chance that you may possibly command someone else's attention long enough to slide yourself in between the tick-tocks of their life, you better be prepared to blow their mind, with who you are and have every right to be.

So if you are not passionate about your idea, product, or service . . . if you are not prepared to WOW people with your enthusiasm, verve, and dynamism . . . if you are not primed to dazzle and enthrall with exuberance aplenty . . . if you are not absolutely, positively, 100 percent ready to stun the civilized world with wonders that will thrill, then expect those whose attention you covet to certainly yawn in your direction.

That is the nightmare of all of us who each night snore with the dream of bliss and success.

Fortunately for all concerned, the Zentrepreneur radiates with a commanding sense of conviction and vision, displaying a personal presence of pizzazz that energizes and creates a moment.

Living a life of passion and purpose, Zentrepreneurs present a positive self-image of spirit, will, and optimism, a belief in themselves that communicates a meaningful and magical quality that can make things happen for themselves and for others.

Zentrepreneurs' passion for doing the work they love, for living the life they dreamed, creates a clarity and power, a brilliant flame that draws people to the source. As a Zentrepreneur, those that you come in contact with will clearly be interested in who you are and what it is that you do. Feeling cheated when you are done, they will want to know more, because since the dawn, humans have always wanted to get close to the fire. Your commitment to your true self, to your dream, will excite and ignite the spark in others, by exhibiting to one and all, through example, that you have chosen to fan the flames of your heart with your soul. This deep connective path of heart and soul in Chinese is called *wang tao*. In plain English, it's called happiness.

And understand this about happiness: It needs no cause.

It is in our DNA, inside each and everyone of us—it is the ultimate dynamic of life. Happiness is part of our *li*—our organic make-up, the balance of spirit and energy that when tapped, spirals serendipitously outward, helping to spin the universe. Discovering and engaging our passion, our natural gifts, talents, and abilities, discovering the secrets to marketing our dream, will open the door to an inexhaustible source of joy in both our personal and professional lives. To live a life of gladness, all any of us have to do is make a conscious decision about the future and the glorious wonders we want to create, realizing that while tragically so many people make the mistake of waiting for happiness, happiness is always here, waiting for us.

It's that simple.

And if only you would come to accept this, maybe you will better the human condition, but then again, maybe you won't. But you will better your own. And nothing wrong with working your side of the street, not one thing wrong at all. Because to reclaim your personal power, to market your dream, you must take charge of your life, reawakening the inner truth of who you are and what you can do.

Attention must be paid to reestablishing a relationship with your spiritual dragon, the glowing persona waiting to activate your internal flame, unleashing your passion for work and the unlimited energy to live an exciting and fulfilling life that reflects your desires and dreams. And riding along side is this: You must validate and affirm boundless belief in your potential to succeed, despite the difficulties and the doubts of others.

Plus one more thing only: SHOW UP!

Pleeease don't just make an appearance in your work and in your life. For every day of living, show up fully, with purpose, passion, commitment, power, intensity, and volume.

Yes, volume.

Live your life out loud! Live every day at a much higher level than you ever imagined possible. Care, and care desperately, about what makes your heart go pitty-pat and what it is that reverberates inside your mind and soul. Deepen your autonomy by embracing the quality of your life, spending your time and energy on whatever it is that moves you. With always increasing determination, push yourself hard and push yourself continually to live out your dream.

In other words, take it to the wall!

We want to cajole, urge, convince you in pursuit of your passion to go way beyond the extra mile. Become speedracers all. Remember to remember now and forever that happiness in work and in life is there, fully accessible, the swirl of it a birthright waiting to be claimed. It is this realization that will keep you from becoming one of those who go through life with noses pressed against the windowpane, watching all the good stuff going on. One of the points to keep is that it is you and you alone that can create your future, through your actions and your attitude. Hoping that this shiny truth lingers prominently in your memory and to put a little historical perspective into this book, let us mention that Aristotle, who only spent more time thinking than any of us about the whole of the human condition, concluded that happiness depends only on ourselves.

And so now, at this your moment of relaxation and reading, Ron and I will ask the most obvious of follow-ups, and this is it: Have you claimed your birthright of happiness? Are you doing the work you love? Are you living your dream? And if not, why not?

Wait—don't answer. Not yet. Take as deep a breath as you can and then summon up the bleak badinage that haunts you. Chances are your noggin is already echoing with excuses . . . Not enough time . . . Not enough money . . . Not enough security . . . Not enough faith . . . Not enough help . . . Not enough connections . . . Not enough knowledge . . . Not enough emotional support. . . .

Whoa.

Jettison these toxic blocking beliefs. Total BS, say we, delicately. The only *enough* that you must attach yourself to for salvation is to possess enough will, enough intensity, and enough power to accept change. Ultimately the happiness in your life and in your work depends on whether you are flexible and responsive enough to go with the unknowns that present themselves day to day. Practicing the present, the Zentrepreneur lets go of the then and there and lives in the here and now.

The secrets to marketing your dream comes when you recognize yourself as being one with the process. Never fearing uncertainty, the Zentrepreneur applies the paradox of certainty, realizing nothing is fixed in place or time. The careful observance of nature teaches us that everything in our experience exists on the edge of perpetuation—sun follows moon, winter follows autumn, creation follows destruction—every minuscule aspect of the universe is nothing but a confluence of movement and change. It is inherent in all things and nothing can escape its operation. Every second, every minute, every hour, every measure of existence is continually in flux. The only thing that is unchanging is change itself. It is the only true continuum.

An ancient Zen koan relates the story about a monk who asked his master to be gracious enough to show him the way. The master said, "Do you see the sky between the branches?" The monk said, "Yes, I do." The master replied, "Here is the way." Zentrepreneurs never try to get the universe to accommodate them, but instead prepare themselves to accommodate the universe, having the grace to make the universe their partner, welcoming the opportunities that are the result of continuing change. Realizing that change *is*.

Quick ramble. Frequently, Ron and I are humbled by the many invitations we receive to come guest lecture and spiel our philosophies and Zentrepreneurial insights to questions on what it takes to be a zest zealot, a passion persister, how to pursue positive possibilities, how to make the spirit of success your constant companion. At one such recent lively seminar, we were asked the following question by an energetic, bright, back-of-the-room attendee who thought he would courteously challenge our idealistic presence with a half-hearted humorous Zen koan of his own. This was his question: "How many Zentrepreneurs does it take to screw in a light bulb?" And here was our answer (which we were without a beat—please believe me—quick to offer); "None. The universe spins the bulb while the Zentrepreneur simply stays out of the way."

The point being that we must realize that the universe is for us and with us, embrace it, without holding on. It is our invitation to partake of infinity. When the Zentrepreneur follows the way of nature, it is therefore possible to respond to change. When the Zentrepreneur understands the design of nature, it is therefore possible to respond to opportunities. It is opportunity that makes our lives vibrant, splendid, and wonderful. Each end is a new beginning. When you breathe in, the infinite possibilities of the universe enter. When you breathe out, the energy that the spiritual dragon represents bellows. The inhale takes care of the exhale, the exhale takes care of itself. This is not ordinary respiration—this is the opening and closing the masters referred to as change. Change is the elixir of life. Stating a simple truth, happiness is ours when we respond and adapt with enthusiasm to changes when they appear.

Drape yourself with that thought.

Because it's waaaaay important that you understand this: Changes in our work, in our life, there is no difference. None. The unvarnished reality is that change is nothing more than the gathering of energy that the universe constantly recycles, allowing for the limitless possibilities that it holds for us. Thousands of years ago Chuang Tzu said, "Go with the flow of things and you will find yourself at one with the mysterious unity of the universe." How true. And we have to throw in this: It's your reaction to change that ultimately determines your success or failure when going about the process of marketing your dream.

The ancients advised us to become better human beings by being like bamboo, dealing with events directly and adapting with endurance to change as need be. While the strongest tree can be uprooted and knocked over in a storm, bamboo prevails in adverse conditions, by bending and yielding to the prevailing winds. Graceful and assured under pressure, bamboo moves easily with the shifts of circumstance, all the while retaining its own innate and effortless strength. The resilience of bamboo can be mirrored in the mind of the Zentrepreneur: Meet sudden changes in life and business with a deposition of vitality and flexibility. Flexibility masters difficulty. Meet change . . . greet change . . . merge with it . . . mold it . . . evolve with it . . . morph with it . . . become harmoniously one with it. Be the change you wish to see. Become the person you were meant to be.

And we want to add this:

Wise Zentrepreneurs know that the most meaningful and rewarding accomplishments are the result of not hanging onto the world that they know.

In other very important words, do not paint your world too small.

On a planet filled with sideshows, make the things you do and the things you want to do the main attraction. Take what you have and have what it takes to make your life an exhilarating opus of radiance for yourself and all those that you come in contact with.

Passion in. Passion out.

As a Zentrepreneur, you are an artist of zest. Your life and your work are the paints and the brushstrokes, the inner portrait that gives your essence its fullest expression. You must banish beige and drabby dull from your life and business palette forever, painting your passion, the picture of your life's work, only in bright primary colors. Again, create an excitement, an exuberance for whatever it is that you bring—an idea, a project, a plan, a product, a service.

Stand up!

Stand out!

Stand ready to make a difference by coloring others with your enthusiasm—thrill them, surprise them, amaze them, make it your mantra to move another human being. Be a performance artist. If you make each effort a masterpiece, know that the gods can do no better.

Listen, post this behind your eyelids: We all want to believe in something, in someone. We are most all of us desperate optimists, waiting for the moon to appear from behind the clouds, hoping for wonders to unfold before us. How else will future anthropologists be able to explain the popularity of Captain Kirk?

The point is this: The majority of those out there are all mentally munching popcorn, with dull and deadened senses—they live humdrum existences as their own movie of life unspools. Waiting for the house lights to come on, they sit there, desperate in the dark, hoping for someone golden to come along to surrender to. By exhibiting your passion, by living your dream, you will become a rock of belief for all who you come in contact with. Your enthusiasm is a contagion, and sharing it creates beneficial, positive energy—*chi*, which will bring strength and good fortune to yourself and others.

That's all it is, this craft of living the life you imagine. By piloting your passion, by specializing in self-optimization, the energy you give will equal the energy you get, allowing you to achieve a more fulfilling and gracious existence. And with this very much in mind, here is as good as spot on the page as any for us to step off the curb, spending a few seconds to offer some beginning crucial advice to marketing your dream, and this is it: When you go out there, and forever on, be at your best.

And sell yourself.

Sell the hell out of yourself.

Know that you can make a difference.

w that you can *be* the difference.

Be committed.

Be enthusiastic.

Be practiced.

Be disciplined.

Be dedicated.

Be dignified.

Be brilliant.

Be humble.

Be vital and vibrant.

Be courageous and calm.

Be brave and daring.

Be trustworthy and honest.

Be cheerful and optimistic.

Be knowledgeable and skilled.

Be positive and determined.

Be inspired and inspiring.

Be appreciative and kind.

Be not for or against.

And as a very strong rule, look up to people and look down on no one.

And mean it.

Using your combination of mind and talent, dazzle and dazzle brilliantly. If an ability to shine is foreign to you, suck it up and give it a shot if you even think about encompassing a work and a life that you care about. Paint your passion, so others may believe. Live your passion, so that you may succeed.

Can you? Will you?

Yes and yes.

Realizing in the end, if you can do anything well, you can do everything well.

JIANYI

Perseverance

Chapter Three
PERSEVERANCE

WEATHERING THE DAZE—
REIGN AND SHINE

The greatness of a dragon is not judged by its strength, but by its perseverance.

Now for your personalized self-marketing forecast. One that you can be sure to count on with absolute certainty:

Do not expect clear skies.

The decision to self-market your dream will cloud you with confusion, thunder you with turmoil, and leave you wading chin-high through doubt pouring down in a torrent. Know now that weathering the daze of disappointment, frustration, and setbacks will not leave you toasty and dry, and it is not (repeat: not) for those individuals with weak mental and emotional resources. To take on the challenges and obstacles of self-marketing your dream, you must have the ability to work from the inside out in all ways, approaching each new day with a presence and consciousness that is catalyzed with patience, persistence, and perseverance. We promise you that no matter how great your intention, how sincere your aspiration, how exceptional your idea, without resolute steadfastness and purposeful determination, you will tangle yourself in nonexistent limitations and knot yourself in unfounded fears. Doomed by your own inaction, you will wimp out, abandoning the richer experience that awaits you, languishing in the repeated echoes of shoulda-coulda, the ultimate phantasm that haunts us all.

Not a good place.

So here is something we would like you to learn today, and it is so important that it can't be overstated: It takes a give-as-good-as-you-got commitment to manifest your vision. More than any specific skill or talent, self-marketing a dream requires placing priority on certain qualities of thought and attitude. Adaptability of thought and action will allow you to overcome seemingly insurmountable setbacks, viewing adversity and failure as only temporary barriers to success. Be unreasonable. Hang on to a tenacity that others may think is an upside-down belief, until the world looks level. Perseverance gives timing a chance to come to your aid. Realize, please, adaptability is not the attribute of a blessed special few—it is the endowment of all who open themselves to inspiration, desire, and hard work.

To be a Zentrepreneur is to understand the essential lesson handed down in Charles Darwin's study, *On the Origin of Species*. Often mistakenly misquoted as expounding the survival of the fittest, truth is, Darwin's theory is actually based on what he described as the "survival of the most adaptable." The true Zentrepreneur adheres to the mantra that the positive force of a pliant attitude is the most powerful source of energy available, allowing you to adapt to circumstance and attend to those things that can be controlled—your thoughts, your emotions, the endless moments of doubt, the self-directness that gives you the endurance to act, excel, and succeed. A really good idea demands it. It also demands that there be a led-and-fed readiness to tolerate uncertainty. To know that there is a way. Understand this: Zentrepreneurs never retreat from their goals. They constantly affirm their conviction that they will find a way to achieve them. And understand this, too: Every single successful product or service that exists was started by a person with an idea and a strong capacity to deliver the idea despite a terrifying tempest of trepidation.

Perseverance is continued effort.

It is also the process of being in love with what you want to do, without being in love with the *idea* of what you want to do. This daze-and-confusion is tragically one of the main reasons that many turn their backs, hopelessly giving in to the pressures of discouragement. Too often too many quit because they believed that their ultimate goal was not reachable, failing to understand that it is the process rather than the product or service that actually gets you there. In other words, it's not the idea that forms the action, it's the action that forms the idea.

Successful people have an enthusiasm for the perpetual experience of the process, which fuels their determination and perseverance, which powers them to do. Loving what you do actualizes a compelling intensity and exuberance that can overcome the damaging intervening thoughts of rejection, uncertainty, and self-pity—thoughts that can, if you let them, paralyze you from taking action. Or worse: cause you to recoil from your purpose. Worse yet: in the crunch, giving up and giving in altogether. The difference between success and failure is the difference between a strong will and a strong won't. Perseverance yields progress. Take solace in Gandhi, who stated that joy lies in the fight.

Perseverance is zest for the pursuit.

It is the willingness to face fear and confront cynicism with a clear-headedness, understanding that success will come when you treat each day of the process as a learning curve rather than an earning curve. Perseverance is the discipline that is used as a review for steps taken, a guide to improve the process with revised insight and dauntless will. It is a way of looking at what needs to be looked at. It is, quite simply, making yourself and your business one percent better in one hundred different ways.

Nutshelling it, it is the courage to forge ahead when you discover the downsides and risks, and fear the inevitable failure. Perseverance is difficult, but it is the hallmark of success. Those that have prevailed in any endeavor have shown a common trait—the endowment of a strong mental spirit. We feel that this can't be repeated too often, which is why we are going to repeat it

again and again throughout this book: The primary attribute available to you in order to successfully market
your dream is ultimately like a gift. . . .

It's the thought that counts.

XINXIN
Faith

Chapter Four
FAITH

THE "F" WORD —
USE IT OR LOSE IT

Those who can see a dragon

are those who believe they can.

It's simple.

The Zentrepreneur's approach to marketing a dream is dependent on creating the moment, having the passion and perseverance to keep going on and on forward, and oh, of course, the Zentrepreneur needs more than the usual amount of intelligence, flexibility, creativity, commitment, tenacity, and a bunch of other good stuff, sure, but in the end, all and every bit of what it takes can still and forever best be summarized in one word only:

Faith.

Not the house-of-worship kind (although if God cursed you and made you a Zentrepreneur, it's all right to go sit in a pew every so often to give thanks). No. What we're talking about here is the written-in-your-heart and on-your-mind kind of faith. Avid faith in your dream, your vision, your talent, and your ability to achieve and succeed. No tip-of-the-tongue, teeter-totter word, faith is the sincere, absolute-yes commitment to building an indomitable spirit and a determined will that allows you to solidify your overall resolution to succeed broadly. When the shadow of doubt covers you and exasperation struggles with you for balance, self-confidence is everything. Confidence and conviction must become a part of your every action and thought. You must be able to sustain yourself against staggering setbacks, unfair reversals, and resounding defeats. Faith is a mind-set, a reservoir of readiness, self-motivation, ambition, training, persistence, and focus. Always and forever never forget that faith in yourself is the greatest power you have and it is, please believe us, a Zentrepreneur's gold mine.

The wise masters agreed that to possess true faith in oneself is to have the strength, wisdom, and courage of ten dragons. Magnificent thought, that. With faith, you will gain the ability to withstand the most difficult times and circumstances. With faith, you will gain the grace, sureness, and confidence of an infinitely superior being, aligning your mind, body, and spirit with your higher Self. With faith you will gain the empowerment to release your abundant potential for expressing your purpose and realizing your best. That being said, in the spirit of fairness and truth-telling, with faith, while there is very much to gain, there is also a lot to lose.

Not a bad thing.

Be thrilled to know that with faith you will lose the anxiety, guilt, and worry over the uncontrollable. With faith, you will lose your skepticism and fear of failure. With faith, you will lose the self-imposed, negative distortions that you are incapable of reshaping yourself and your life.

By affirming your faith in your self, your idea, concept, product, or business, you will be able to turn what the ancient Buddhists called the Wheel of Becoming, where the interdependence of one thing on the next perpetuates the movement of the wheel, propelling you more aggressively and persistently forward. Your abilities, achievements, and potential will crush and grind to dust the obstacles, doubts, and negative elements that await you on your challenging path ahead.

Now you must believe this. You must wake up every morning of the world and believe that keeping the faith is so important to successfully marketing your dream. And do you want to know why? Quick clue:

Because there are monsters out there.

Dream-killers. Career-cripplers. Wow-wreckers. Success-suckers. Horrible, merciless, callous creatures that spew a toxic, tormenting nightmare of negativity and doom. Naysayers who will look at you strangely, and they will say such killingly hard, terrible things as:

—It's a stupid idea.

—It can't be done.

—You're not going to make it

—Don't take the chance.

And frankly, why they are that way, we don't get it. But there is one thing that we do want for you to get, and that is, just as quickly as you can, away.

As fast as your nifty little Nike ground-grippers will take you, you must distance yourself from those prophets of doom who will pull you from your purpose, drain your energy, lay waste your ambitions, and crush your spirit. To keep their company is to risk squandering your spark or, worse even still, risk their throttling your beloved dream until it goes dead bouncing. You must leave them there, trapped in their own persona. Their negativity is their problem—don't let them make it yours because it will always be easier for them to pull you down rather than you lift them up.

Now the following is just for you, so please pay close attention.

Like glue, you must affix yourself to like-minded people—people of goodwill who will support you and not pound you with discouragement when shadows come to stay. Just as birds of a feather flock together, people of confidence cluster, and if you're lucky (and never forget that you are), you can attach yourself to such people who have positive attitudes and are excited about your uniqueness and the growth you want to see in your life. They can be your Yoda and help you maintain faith in your idea and in who you are and what you are capable of accomplishing, the destiny you will shape.

We cannot overemphasize the importance of a supportive someone at the start, when it comes to marketing your dream. Because faith can also appear as a friend, a giant on whose shoulders you can stand. Someone who can help you see over the horizon with brimming vitality, where possibilities can become probabilities. Someone like yourself who even under the darkest cloud sees a sunny day with undiminished optimism. This is important because a Zentrepreneur's truest test is to let belief loose in the land. So treat those who have placed their faith in you with kindness unending. Because as you take on the hour-by-hour daily challenges and all the related stresses and strains, the dips and slides of marketing your dream, what is one friend worth?

You decide. . . .

GEXING

Individuality

Chapter Five

INDIVIDUALITY

WHEN TO PLAY—
PLAY TO WIN

The ascent of a dragon into heaven

is a majesty beyond compare.

Make a miracle? Nothing to it really.

Just head on over to the Holy Land, get yourself to the mountaintop, and with fingers very much crossed, seek a favor from the Burning Bush. Or more impossible still yet, gather up all your energy, talent, skill, and expertise, knock on a bunch of doors trying as hard as you know in hopes that whoever answers will miraculously fall in love with what you bring. Either way, remember where you parked. Because rejection, more often than not, rules the day. And as you lick your wounds in despair doing the windshield time back to the comfort and sanctuary of your pit, this much will be clear and obvious:

You aren't ready.

Oh, we understand you are totally a pro and very much charming and winning, probably careful to smell nice and look full-well spiffy in your appearance, too. But what is it about you, your idea, your product, service, or business that is so fresh and different, so splendidly special that it will let light into the world? What is it about opening your Pandora's box that will fill the moment?

While you're at it, explain why you feel that what you have to offer in today's hyper-competitive market is not cookie-cutter, plain Jane, conveyor-belt standard? Really take a minute or so to genuflect. How is what you do or say goes way far beyond expectations to create the emotional magic that keeps those whose attention you favor from snoozing in their chairs?

Think, fellow Zentrepreneurs.

Think real hard.

Please, do us a favor and crank it over in your mind. We'll wait for you a few lines down the page, knowing that if you iris in to embrace the honest answer, again this much will be clear and obvious:

You aren't ready.

At least that's our guess.

What we're talking about here is not to expend time imagining what *might happen* as a result of your effort, but rather imagine what it is that *you can actually make happen* as a result of your effort. By integrating focus and purpose, you can direct energy into action. By engaging persistence and determination, you can make the transition from idea to reality.

You must believe that everyone and everything have their own unique possibilities. It doesn't matter if what you have to offer isn't earth-shaking new. Likewise if what you have or bring has the marvelous ability to change lives and shoot the moon—same thing. Doesn't matter. What does matter is that once you've made up your mind embracing an intention to get into the game and play, you absolutely must arc it with an ambition and intention to win, by showing all that what you represent and come swinging with is so totally (drum roll, please) D-I-F-F-E-R-E-N-T.

An example: going back a bit through years past, back to when the Republic of Tea began entertaining the possibility of launching its exceptional line of gourmet, varietal and bottled teas, soft-drink woolly mammoths still plodded the land. Huge beverage conglomerates were filling luggy-looking bottles with sweetened, unpalatable, laboratory concoctions and peddling it mercilessly by the millions of cases to the unwitting as refreshing, good-for-you iced tea. It was for Ron and me a sadness too bleak to bare. Here was a treasure of the world—the magnificent cup of humanity that began as a medicine, grew into a beverage, was valued as a currency, helped to establish social order, and had been the fundamental touchstone of serenity, peace, and civilized living for five millennium.

Its history of spirit had been scribed and recorded, offering testament to a cultural synthesis that represents a vanguard of human existence: high ideals, religion, morality, aesthetics, philosophy, discipline, and social interaction. Tea was the world's favorite beverage, but alas, the magic and vividness of it were being deluded and diminished into nothing more than dreadful, artificially processed, colored swill. Ignoring the certain wisdom of the *Tao Te Ching* that admonishes to make a small thing great, a great thing had been reduced to an insignificant littleness, and marketed to the masses by those who practiced only occasional attempts at quality. Mankind has done worse, but this was an awfulness so maddening that it stretched our sensibilities and perforated our core. Something had to be done.

So we began.

Inspired by the burgeoning success of our Tea Revolution, Ron declared, as the premier merchants of only the finest teas in the world, it was our responsibility to deliver men, women, and children everywhere to a bottled beverage that engendered the spirit, art, and ideals of true tea. It was going to be a staggering mission—there was to be a quenchless thirst for perfection and new thresholds had to be met. It would be an enormous undertaking that would take time, persistence, and a deep commitment to our purpose, but no matter. We took our charge seriously.

Very.

Victor Hugo once counseled, "That an invasion of armies can be resisted but not an idea whose time has come." The more Ron and I shared our missive whisperings about the powerful idea to create a bottled tea to be elevated to its rightful place beside fine wine, the more we wanted to shout our excitement to the world.

For tea is like wine. From one plant, the *Camellia sinensis*, comes many teas, while one species, *Vitis vinifera*, is responsible for nearly all the wine in the world. As it is with wine grapes, so it is with tea. The two are running parallel. Both are masterpieces of agricultural art, a product of its cultivation—the subtle differences of the soil, the elevation, the climate, the sunshine, the rain, drought, the whims of the weather, from one harvest to another, all affect the character of the tea leaf and grape. While wine intoxicates, tea exhilarates. And enchants.

And captures the mind.

Going out to dine? Order a bottled varietal tea, not wine. As the two of us toiled, let me tell you that imaginations whirred at the possibilities the idea revealed. *Chajins*, tea masters, would stand tableside at Spago or The Four Seasons, offering a refreshing realm of leafy flavors to be paired with food, suggesting the glories of light-, medium-, or full bodied teas, with talk of "peak" and "finish," which is best with risotto, which goes good with lamb or is recommended to accompany shellfish. The thought of introducing a gulping nation to the extraordinary experience of sipping a consistent beautifully balanced beverage that clears the mind and palate, cools and delights the tongue, and would compliment fine food brilliantly made us giddy with visions of tuxedoed sommeliers sent running to spray their corkscrews with WD-40 to keep the rust from forming.

The picture should be coming clear. We weren't out to create another iced tea offering. We were going to be the protagonists to create an entirely new category. A phenomenon. We were going to design an eye-catching, WOW package. We were going to craft a wondrous, WOW taste experience. We were going to bring into being a WOWerful, brewed iced tea that was to set hearts aflutter. We were going to become a raging tempest of evolutionary revolutionaries. We were going to amaze, surprise, rock, jolt, jar, freak, come mightily forward, and show one and all that what we were about to throw down and unleash was something that was going to be so bold, soooooo wildly DIFFERENT.

Erasmus said, "Fortune favors the audacious." With that in mind, hold your breath, folks . . . presenting the clarity and the beauty of the first, all-natural, unsweetened, gourmet, varietal, bottled iced teas!

And, yes, it was going to be a breath-holding crapshoot, and, my God, was it without question ever to be a daring-do, humongous risk, and riding right along side keeping those colossal constants company was the ever-present thought that horrendous financial calamity could cover us all. Still, as Zentrepreneurs, we knew that the true path is always paved with challenges and jeopardy, sure. But let us have at it.

However, as terrific as the concept was, could we pull this baby off? Could we create such a thing?

Or worse.

What if after all the tremendous effort and expense, no one noticed it? Or much more worse yet, what if on that sunshine, blue morning we woke up to discover the shock that not one single person on planet Earth cared?

We could be talking bottled Edsel here.

Enough with the suspense. What's important for you to know is that the very first review came out of the *Arizona Daily Star* and it went like this:

> Your breath hitches in anticipation, your heart races. Your waiter is removing the top from the curvaceous bottle, pouring some of the precious liquid into a glass. He swishes it around and passes it beneath your nose. Ah, the bouquet of Blackberry Sage. And then the taste. There couldn't be a finer tea. Tea? My dear, where have you been? The Republic of Tea has begun distributing brewed teas in bottles to restaurants that care. A bit pricey perhaps, but you're worth it.

Within days, more kind words like that quickly followed. Praise unending from the folks at *Food & Wine*, *Cuisine*, *San Francisco Chronicle*, *The New York Times*, *Chicago Tribune*, *Good Morning America*, CNN, and on and on, and blessedly on once again as more plaudits arrived when the bottled teas were given The Clear Choice

Award, Best New Packaging Design Award, and Best New Beverage Product of the Year. The point is not to keep you all gathered around this campfire boring you by summoning up such storytellings of success. The point is, please believe me, an important one, which is precisely why it must be mentioned again, and it is this:

Whatever your talent, idea, product, business, or service, whatever it is that you have or bring, you must commit to setting your compass to amaze anew by showing all that you are somehow in some way D-I-F-F-E-R-E-N-T.

Overwhelmingly so.

Personal aside:

I don't watch a lot of television. Lately I don't think that there's much of any value whatsoever to watch as the occasional attempts at quality become more rare. But when I do sit back, taking control of the clicker, like an increasing number of viewers, I find myself flocking to cable TV's Food Network. A sinful admission, but I must confess I am a sucker for the crunchy competition of the oh-so-popular *Iron Chef* program. And if you were to ask me to enter a plea regarding a propensity for the fancy sauces of Mario Batali or the in-your-face style of Bobby Flay, I would admit to being culpable. Likewise, if I have to stand trial for admitting to being hooked on the daily offerings and exhilarated outbursts of chef

Emeril Lagasse, then so be it, I plead guilty to the pleasure, so take me away. But here's an example that is so important for you to take away.

A few years back the pretty much unknown Emeril Lagasse was a nomad, invisibly wandering his kitchen in New Orleans. But that was then. Now he has become the crowd pleaser that he is by parlaying the same old ingredients into a splendid rehash. He possesses a successful financial portfolio of books, restaurants, and a multitude of products worth many millions to be sure, all which have come his way by shouting "BAM!" and "Kick it up a notch." He had the brilliance and the passion to know that sharing recipes wasn't going to be the way for him to breakout and slingshot himself to the top of the food chain. He needed to market the dream he had for himself differently. How? By showing the world that he was DIFFERENT, by devoting a focused attention to his personal packaging, by reaching out and serving up the magnificent entertaining *difference* that he knew would set him apart, Emeril has become what he had dared dream of becoming—blessed beyond belief.

And so can you.

If you are only willing to begin the process.

Which is very simple. Simple if you are brave enough to realize that this can be at the same time the hardest step to take of all. Especially if you've been doing what you've been doing for a while.

There is a Zen parable about a monk who asks his master how to enter the path toward enlightenment. "Enter the stream," the master said. "How?" asked the monk. The master admonished, "There is no how. Only now."

True wisdom.

Truer guidance.

Know this: To journey the path of success, it doesn't matter where you are or where you have been. The marvel of the pilgrimage is that it has only to do with where you are going.

And to get there, you need only start right where you are.

In the present.

While many tend to want to wait to begin at just the right time or in just the right place, it is this egregious tendency that is the reason that most never even begin at all. Stop waiting for permission. You were born with the permission to be yourself. In other words, whether you are gearing up anew or have been slaving away in business, doing the work for yourself or somebody else, realize, please, before you can move others, you must first move yourself.

Follow Ron and Stuart's **LAW** (Love And Will)— Love what you do—And—Will yourself to do it.

Your life must have a work experience that is, above all else, personally meaningful for you, one that provides you with a loftiness of purpose, a *want to*—not *a have to*—attitude. Your work must be something about which you care deeply and are enthusiastic, a work that, cloudy or sunny, brings joy to your days. Your work must be a vehicle for the deepest aspirations of your soul and, most importantly, something through which your talents can find full expression. If you do what you like and like what you do, you will never work a day in your life. And we promise you this: You will look forward to all your Mondays with a fabulous feel in the air.

What a wonderful world if every man and woman would connect with this attitude. So with this in mind, if you want, here's the way for you to achieve a work that provides you with exactly such bliss—

But only if you have the courage.

Ready for the answer? Good, the envelope, please.

And here it is—

BE WHAT YOU ARE!

There. The not-so secret's out.

And before you go rolling your eyes, realize that many, maybe most, live lives never realizing their creative potential, gamely going through the motions, forsaking their true gifts, abilities, and dreams because of, sadness of sadness, the pressure placed upon them by others. You simply must not let someone else's expectations for you become your reality. This is your life we are talking about here. YOU ARE IN CHARGE!

You are the one who makes the choice of how you will experience life. In order to achieve and succeed you must not let anyone pull you off your true path, away from your deserved hopes and ambitions. Listen to your heart and believe in your ability to author a meaningful work, resist the strong pressure from family and friends that may be preventing you from opportunities for personal fulfillment and achievement. Again, a Zentrepreneur gravitates towards positive people and situations, seeking out those who will support and inspire, cutting away from those who discourage, distract, drain, or undermine, knowing that to move on, sometimes the best light for the journey can be the result of a burning bridge.

Repeated for emphasis—

BE WHAT YOU ARE!

Dive headfirst into being and know why you are here on this earth. Be awake to what you are and what you can do. Each and every day, in pursuit of your purpose, best apply your energy and talents that will help bring about the changes you would like to realize. Lock yourself into the heroic mold of creating a plan of action to make the transition from what you are doing now to what you ultimately want to do and accomplish. This is what distinguishes a hero from the rest—a hero seeks to take action—to do, to be. Throw open your inner window and look at your ability, credibility, and your marketability. Take a huge magnifying glass and closely and meticulously assess your adequacy to choose, to change, to achieve. Do you have what it takes and can you take what you have to effectively advance and market your dream? Do you have the necessary confidence and possess the knowledge and skills, the self-reliance to brave the obstacles and challenges that await you? If not, then bust a move. Don't wait. Act! It's never too late to become what you could have been.

Again, start where you are.

Do the intellectual spadework and legwork required. Begin to accumulate the wisdom, support, and the assistance needed to succeed in marketing your dream. You don't have to have a Ph.D. or be an MBA maven in order to triumph in business. Check out the Forbes 400 list. Among the members of today's big-buck club, there are many high school and college dropouts who have achieved a state of blissful largess by foregoing a college sheepskin, choosing instead to enroll in the even more challenging school of hard knocks. This is something that even the cerebral folks at Cornell University would have to admit to. After all, their founder Ezra Cornell never graduated from any school. In fact, according to a recent report from the Cambridge-based Forrester Research, 20 percent of America's millionaires have never even stepped foot into a college classroom. Nonetheless, to a person, they all reached their fullest potential and were able to live their dream because, more than anything else, they committed to the science of success. In other very important words, they were all willing to learn. How important. A Chinese master resolved, "If you plan for one year, plant rice. If you plan for ten years, plant trees. If you plan for a hundred years, educate yourself."

Be open to new knowledge, live your passion, set goals, take risks, find a mentor, choose to be happy, do all the things that we covered in our companion book, *Success at Life* (which hopefully you read and how dare you not). Prepare, prepare, prepare. Graciously, honor your innate strengths, gifts, and talents, passionately embracing the difference that you can make. Zentrepreneurs must boldly take the steps necessary to fulfill their vision. To affect success at creating a business and marketing your dream, you must possess the attitudes and experience that will separate you into those who possess a dragon's wings and soar with success from those who tailspin and spiral to Earth. Expose your dream to the sunlight and see where it fades, never forgetting that in order for someone else to believe in the excitement and the potential of what you are polishing, you have to believe in it first. With desire, dedication, and perseverance, the vision you see will become what can be.

Conceive. Believe. Achieve.

It was Emerson who wrote, "What lies behind us and what lies before us are tiny matters compared to what lies within us." This is in line with the Tao that decreed if you cultivate the inner self, your power becomes real. When we are true to our inner selves we act in concert with the rightness of our dreams and visions. We become the difference we wish to create. Only by reaching this illumined level of honesty can we fulfill our own nature and influence the nature of others.

Shakespeare wrote, "Look with thine ears." As Zen-trepreneurs, know that the true consciousness of those you court is the result of looking with ears and listening with eyes. To be a merchant of vision is important now crucially more than ever in our medium-is-the-message society. While most people understand we create an impression through, clothing, hairstyle, speech patterns, and body language, many are clueless to the fact that something as overlooked as a business card, letterhead, envelope, or Web banner can carry just as much weight, maybe even more, since it is initially and instantly a way for you to cut yourself from the herd and stand out from the morass of material people are horsewhipped with everyday. Which is why it is crucial for you to make more than a concerted effort to creatively construct your personal signage. For starters, how about a business card that matters? Which is also the reason why we would like to take a few beats here to inject a nugget and make an example out of this so often ho-hum, neglected first sign of you.

Now before you go throwing the book across the room, we promise you in the scheme of things, an effective, carefully crafted business card is an important defining vehicle, as important and as essential as anything you may try to do in achieving your more-than-a glance, attention-gaining goal. Hard to believe, we know. True though. Successful Zentrepreneurs understand that their business card is one of their most diamond-bright, strategic marketing tools. It's their Nike swoosh, their Jordan smile, it's the confident, cool pride of place that reflects the difference of who they are. It's also the flame and fizz they leave behind.

Plato pronounced, "The beginning is the most important part of the work." Such suchness was also expressed in the Tao: "Big things in the world can be accomplished by seeing to their small beginnings." Now this isn't a strict rule, but more often than not we think it's true—when you create a business card, you are setting up your universe. When you present your business card, you are letting someone know the very world they're invited to enter. Your world. A special world, remember, that offers a sense of purpose, passion, and excitement. And just in case you went to the kitchen to glom a snack, and because we can't repeat this too often or too strongly, a world that is for all to see D-I-F-F-E-R-E-N-T.

A whole lot to demand from a piece of pulp that measures only two by three and half inches.

With over 50 billion business cards printed in the United States every year, we urge you to do yourself a favor and pony up the bucks for a clever graphic designer to orchestrate for you an attention-engaging, powerful visual statement about you, your product, service, or business. Maybe you won't believe this, but we do: Your business card is your personal packaging. Like Madonna's entrance, it is the visual dressing that determines to a certain extent how the public relates to you. It's the ground you are asking them to put their feet on. With so much at stake, the design of your visual identity is best entrusted to an experienced, talented professional. Try to green light yourself an accomplished graphic designer who has created logos and stationery for other small companies or entrepreneurs, one who can create a visibility program of promotional and marketing materials that are just the right image for you.

Remember that when it comes to all aspects of business, expertise and talent don't cost, they pay!

So learn to embrace design.

Obsess design.

Define it.

Decide on it.

Deliver it.

Connect yourself with the idea that design is the Rosetta stone that will influence and guide your target customer to what you represent and offer. Design creates a consciousness-raising connection that can solidify you with your public. In a visual society, design communicates in a way that words cannot. Swallow hard and spend some of your beginning budget on design.

That's the first step in this very important investment in yourself and very much worth whatever dollars a local graphic design service might charge. A well thought-out, communicative visual design is one of the most ad-hered-to mantras of business success. Every physical representation of your business image that appears, all of your visual format, from invoice to letter, brochure to banner, every collateral material offers an opportunity to make an extra impression and successfully shape and control communicative impact to your customer. This is an obvious yet ignored fact: There are 400,000 words in the English language, yet things that people see do affect them more. Powerful, pleasing images can move them. It can put perceived value in your product or service. You can bet the farm on this—the value of an effective, stand-out, positive image will go a long, loaded-dice way in declaring your difference and helping you win the battle for hearts and minds.

"The Republic of Tea's teapot logo anchors the company's numerous expressions of its identity to its vision. The company markets its teas by variety and by the tea drinkers' preferences. It promotes its teas by creating a unique ambiance, presented in a letter from the 'Minister of Travel.' The teapot logo can take various forms, with the steam issuing from its spout implying different personalities and moods."   —from *Designing Business: Multiple Media, Multiple Disciplines,* by Clement Mok

Now maybe this never occurred to you, but because success and failure always run neck and neck, such attention to overlooked stuff like this will give you the rooting interest that can very well help make things magical. Make your glimmering become fact.

And maybe might allow you to win.

And bless your life and work with fun and joy.

Because that is what success must ultimately bring. Fun and joy and the realization that:

1. When you stop having fun and joy, you stop winning.

2. When you stop having the confidence to know that you are the person to create a difference, you stop winning.

3. When you stop pursuing your potential and passion, you stop winning.

4. When you stop expressing your unique self through your product or services, you stop winning.

5. When you stop understanding that success comes to those who grasp it, you stop winning.

6. When you stop having the confidence to know that you are the person to create a difference, you stop winning. (Same as number two but we think it needs repeating.)

7. When you stop accomplishing something meaningful and significant, you stop winning.

This amazingly is anathema to the gray flannels of the world who have decreed that winning is to be measured by salary, benefits, title, prestige, recognition, that the remunerative rewards of wealth and goods are the critical criteria for keeping score and are the measure of career. Like the *Godfather*, it's business—it's not personal. How so very wrong. Business is personal. Or it had better be. That's the best basic advice. Challenging work, work for which you are naturally gifted, is essential to your well-being and the well-being of the world, offers spiritual as well as material fortification, and allows for one's creative expression that results in a desired outcome—that's meaningful livelihood. The underlying truth, the ultimate reality is that there's more to life then the drudgery of performing uninspiring daily tasks in order to pay down your Visa card. Being true to your heart is what is genuinely going to count in the end. It's the one thing that echoes.

But you have to be a player.

Followed hard by, you have to play to win.

Play with a positive expectancy of success. Act and think like someone who can bring it home every time. Having the courage to do, to be, to play the game of life and career with heartiness and a buoyancy, to rise up and ride your inner dragon when others expect you to fail will bring you the ultimate euphoria of success. Doesn't matter if you are currently running a business, or if you're ready to go at it out there alone. Matters not one bit. What does matter is that you specialize in self-optimization, with the explicit objective of succeeding through your passion, talents, and gifts. Make the extra effort that can make your work an affirming art. When self-marketing your dream, show that what you do because of you is DIFFERENT. Hate to lose more than you love to win. Raise your game by ratcheting up your performance and skills. Each and every time you step up to the plate, swing away with a surge of confidence that will allow you to endure. And win.

What we're trying to throw in here is that confidence is the key to unlocking your potential. Passion, talent, and ability are all terrifically part of the spice in your stew, but in order to be a true Zentrepreneur you must also have the confidence to act. The basic challenge facing us all is to do whatever it takes to achieve our goal. Any success you will achieve will come only as a result of an action you undertake. Failure to act is the difference between success and failure. As a Zentrepreneur, know that even if you are on the right path you will still lose your way if you don't move forward. You must (underline: <u>must</u>) meet and greet each new day and all of your days that follow as a committed player in the cause of a deeper, richer experience for yourself. Protect your destiny, your greatness, and your hope. Don't just go with life, grow with life. Feed your mind, support your spirit continually with positive thoughts. There's no way of stating it any clearer, but this might come close—

You have to think you can.

When presenting the first snippets of this book, our very great and good-hearted publisher was gracious enough to ask Ron and me for our thoughts and input on how to best categorize the book: Business, self-help, inspirational, motivational—what? What say we to which shelf should be targeted for our precious and hard-worked little glory to be placed on? An important discussion for lots of reasons. Mostly because no one wants what we've put down to be invisible. People who know their objective should not have to go wandering through their neighborhood bookseller searching with hope.

Hmmm. . . .

Want to read one of the greatest self-help, inspirational, motivational books on business ever? Originally published in 1937, chances are someone gave it to you long ago and it's no longer among your possessions, although it should be. This is the book that was your first lesson in positive thinking and self-confidence, and a book that should occupy a sacred spot of its own on every business, self-help, inspirational, motivational book shelf anywhere, but sadly it doesn't. Still most stores do carry it treating it with care. Go pick up *The Little Engine That Could,* by Watty Piper, illustrated by Christina Ong. Make it required reading and revisit its pages often. I took a little time to read it again today, and at the oh-so-slim risk of becoming a crummy spoilsport, ruining the splendid ending for three or four of you, let me tell you that while the doomed-to-fail, shiny new engine and strong engine are a choir of such intense hopelessness, "I cannot. I cannot," the shtoonk-of-a-nothing Little Blue Engine overcomes insurmountable odds to deliver the train of toys over the mountain with the resolute mantra: "I think I can . . . I think I can . . . I think I can."

Proving only once again, that hope is where you find it. No matter what anybody says. . . .

CHUANBU
Word of mouth

Chapter Six
WORD OF MOUTH

BANG A GONG—
GET A BUZZ ON

When word of a dragon came,

all sought out its existence.

What a thing.

With great care, you've prepared properly. Giving as good as you got, you planned and plotted. Leaving no stone on earth unturned, you slogged over every detail, making the dream for your business twinkle, as you went about in agony, of course, scraping together every possible dollar, borrowing what you could borrow, hoping that because of your wisdom, skill, and luck, your Website will get a hit, or your phone will ring, or your door will swing open, knowing with a certain confidence, if you will just do all that you can do, the fates will deliver you to the magic moment and splendor you've glamorized over and over. You're sure of it.

Don't hold your breath.

The truth? Total wipeout disaster because, more often than not, your Website will not get downloaded, your phone will go silent, and no crowds will come flocking to your door. The demons have tricked you. And the sheer calamity of it will be shocking and painful and that will only be the beginning of the Armageddon that will take its horrible mental hold, as you spend your mourning period trying to control your crumbling world, cursing your helplessness, voicing the standard entrepreneur operatic whine: If only there had more money or more time or more of whatever resources it takes to get what you offer to the masses—or the masses to what you offer. But by very much then, providing your heart holds up, you will be a whisper away from oblivion, and not a lot else.

And if by very good chance, the above is cause for your enthusiasm to be stopped cold, your mind to go spinning away to some dark place to hide, then here is as good a place as any to spotlight the absolute, unembellished, success dynamic of any business big or small, and it is a paramount proviso so we are going to put it in very large type:

YOU MUST HAVE A CUSTOMER!

Okay, we understand the duh-worthiness of so obvious a truism. However, was it also so obvious to you and worthy of your attention to face squarely when you created your operating budget? When the monies were allocated did the monthly expenditure reflect some marketing jack to spread the word about what you offer or do, or was what you came up with when you went digging nothing but dry dust? A concern, yes, but not very. So often the path of reality is the one most often overlooked, a problem endemic to many entrepreneurial disasters, which is why you must take to heart and heed the following:

More important than your business idea, more important than your service or product, more important than the salaries, computers, phones, rent, lights, equipment, loans, more important than any and all of it is the important importance of attracting, getting, and keeping customers.

Solid enough, obvious, sure, since it is the customer money that in the end pays for it all.

An aside to all start-ups: Forget self-imagined assumptions such as, "If you build it, they will come." Directions are needed. You must consciously go after the customer, the client, the prospect, the subscriber, the member. An old Chinese proverb says, "A business hidden in shade never enjoys the sun." You must pursue, convey, pique, attract, engage, excite, and motivate the movement to what you offer. The miracle (not too strong a word) of success for any business is the impulse that compels people to your company, product, or service. End of aside.

We want to pause a bit now for a basic truth that needs explaining.

Here is one of the main rules of marketing we want you to know: Advertising is expensive. PR, too. Most agencies won't even share their breathing space with you if you do not have a weekly-monthly advertising budget with thousands solidly chunked away.

Here is another marketing rule that you need to know: No matter how much money you spend or how often you spend it, you're clutching at vapor. Reason? Information overload. Advertising so constantly bombards our senses on a daily basis that we have learned to block it out. Media ads get lost in the clutter. Print ads lose their absorbency when you turn the page. The customer is more cynical and more distrusting of advertising than ever before, not really paying attention as they did in the past and no longer trusting the message. Research now indicates that only 50 percent of all advertising works and it only works 50 percent of the time.

So, if we were to tell you that for not a whole lot of spending money there are much more surer, on-a-shoe-string ways to attract the business you covet, you would probably protest (you would be wrong, but you're entitled). At any rate, here is the most important, cavalry-to-the-rescue rule of marketing that you must come to know:

Buzz is better.

The invisible influence of word of mouth is one of the most powerful and effective, low-cost marketing strategies that can deliver you and your business to the attention of your target audience more consistently than any advertising campaign can ever promise to do, no matter how many dollars are spent. Statistics show that consumers are overwhelmingly persuaded to act based on the recommendations or encouragements of family, friends, colleagues, or buzz. Street talk, Internet chat, guerrilla marketing, the praises of Aunt Betsy or neighbor Norm, sung to others about what you have or do, this is all an integral part of marketing your dream. Yet few start-ups know how the phenomenon of buzz works or how to get it to work.

But, shhhhh . . . we've got secrets.

Every Zentrepreneur does. First things first, let's close in.

What is buzz?

Buzz is a grapevine, word-of-mouth, word-of-press force that no sane person can ignore. It imbues and elevates an aura of wonderment into the minds of multitudes, about a company, product, or service. It can turn a first-time, shaky, out-of-pocket, low-budget movie called *The Blair Witch Project* into a $250 million blockbuster. It can create soaring demand for PT Cruisers and sensational sales of Razor Kick Scooters. It can take a clever and simple piece of song-swap software invented by college roommates and turn it into the most successful technology introduction of all time, the once-upon-a-time 80-million-user, online darling named Napster. The tsunami of it, all done up and delivered without any life-empowering endorsements from Michael Jordan or Oprah. Yet magazines fought to put the stealth chatter of it all on their covers.

So you see, miracles do happen every day.

Kind of.

In order to seed and build buzz, it's essential to begin with a product or service well worth talking about. One that engages and excites the users so that they themselves become the sales force moving others to jump on the bandwagon. To generate successful buzz, what you have to hold out and offer up must have the absolute, all-important power to cure disease—the disease of familiarity. Familiarity will not create buzz. Familiarity only cripples growth. And it can kill a business. Business that is not intrinsically innovative or special is just busy-ness. It is the vocation of those who love to wave their arms and pretend—"Look Ma, I'm in business."

We cannot explain too often how crucial it is for you to commit to being a champion of change. A wizard of wonders. A master of magnificence. A wager of wow. A dean of deliverance. What you must do better then anyone else on earth is create a clear distinction that zeroes in on yourself as being something (here it comes again) D-I-F-F-E-R-E-N-T. Incredibly different and fresh in the way that your product or service goes beyond the usual and exceeds the expectations of those you are attempting to reach. Your customers must experience this difference, be struck by the encountering, if they are to stand up and give a positive testimonial that impacts. Do something outrageously wonderful for your customer. Do it with verve and flair. Turn yourself inside out on behalf of them. Be exemplary. General rule: exceeding expectations—good buzz; falling below expectations—bad buzz.

Which brings us to this question: Does buzz always work?

Never or always.

That's what we think is the answer because contagious buzz, buzz that stimulates discussion and propagates, absolutely demands the involvement of users that are so happily impressed with their encounter and experience that with the zeal of a true believer they talk up their satisfaction with others. In order for buzz to be successful, it must take on the characteristics of a giant snowball, massing, gaining size and weight through the accumulation of interested and involved consumers. The more satisfied they are, excited into responses such as, "Hey, check this out, you got to have this," or "You ought to see that," the more it will create the type of conversational pathway that allows for the exchange of information that introduces, impresses, and influences others, because it is uncoerced, free of any self-interest other than the joy that comes from sharing the discovery and spreading the word of something that delighted.

Questions for you: Where do you go for counsel regarding a car repair? Who do you ask about whether purchasing a Palm Pilot is something that's for you? How do you find out about a great restaurant, club, or movie? Or who out there is good enough to cut your hair? You ask a friend, a neighbor, or peer, welcoming their suggestions, respecting their suggestions.

Buzz is not motivated by personal gain, but is roused by the satisfaction of helping friends, colleagues, or like-minded individuals find great products or services. Buzz is the marketing message that emanates from the most efficacious endorser possible—the customer. The operative word in that sentence is customer. It is customers that have us in their power, at their mercy. You may live above the store, but it is they who have the ability to flick the switch on your open or closed sign. Understand: Buzz is all powerful because it is the language of the customer, not the seller. For many, buzz is the truth.

But it is up to you to make it happen.

It is you who must be the relentless architect that supplies the building blocks of buzz that your business will have to stand on. It is you who will be responsible for making sure it will not crumble the moment the weight of reality is applied. There is a formula for creating good buzz, and you must be the active ingredient. Which brings us to this: Is your product or service ready? More importantly, again, are you ready? Ready to switch to an igniter mind-set and spark the energy of buzz that can catalyze your dream to the forefront of your audience?

Then, handle with flair.

Building a successful buzz campaign hinges on walking the talk and seeking the right carriers for your message. Target in on exactly who your potential customers are. A Zentrepreneur knows that you need not look too far. An ancient Zen sutra admonishes, "Clouds are in the sky. Water is in the well." That much is still true. Every industry, community, organization, club, and social circle has conferences, meetings, get-togethers, and speaking opportunities. This is where you will find the opinion makers, chieftains, pooh-bahs—the hives of buzz bees, the powerful, potential cross-pollinators of your message that can take the powdery residue and blossom buzz, spreading the word to yet more carriers, and they in turn to more conversational carriers still. And even if you are a linguistically impoverished King of the Doofus or Queen of the Dweebs, it is your responsibility to leap to the head of the class and promote your wares to anyone who will listen and perhaps buy.

The *I Ching* advises, "It furthers one to have someplace to go." A Zentrepreneur knows that in order to master your comfort zone, you have to learn to leave it. Marketing your dream has always got to be an act of exploration. So get out there and everywhere, and gutsily start talking with people about your product or service. It is you who has to birth your dream. Realizing it's in the telling, that it breathes and grows. This is a reality you must live with every day of your life.

We should add this here: Confucius wrote, "The nature of people is the same—it is their habits that separate them." How true. Your success is not determined by luck, it's determined by the actions you choose to take each and every day. We know this.

And we believe this: Successful people are willing to do the things that unsuccessful people are not willing to do.

Which is where you come in.

You must always be willing to put forth all the energy, effort, time, money, stamina, and skill that you can convoke in order to successfully market your dream. Be incredibly committed to targeting your audience and doing all that you can to reach them and beam your existence. Remember you're not telling a story, *you are the story*. Take the all-important advantage of developing the personality and image of your business. Become a tireless and knowledge-able, passionate speaker. Make sparks fly. Cause people's pulses to change. Transport all who you come in contact with beyond the ordinary and mundane. With clarity and courage, bring awareness, grace, and excellence to their world. Do this without any fear or hesitation—there is no vat of boiling tar waiting for you. Instead, there may very well be the proverbial pot of gold.

A quick riff of an example:

Ron's a road runner. Not the Wile E. Coyote kind, but a marathon man. He runs end to end the twenty-six miles of the Boston, the Chicago, and the others, doing it for many challenging reasons, but doing it most of all for the healthy trifecta of mind, body, and spirit. To help give him the physical energy to brave the rigors of running, Ron (no fool he) like many endurance athletes, takes advantage of the performance-enhancing, winning nutrition offered up in a PowerBar.

While many of you may have noticed that the PowerBar has been a grocery, health food, and convenience store staple for some years now, what you may not know is that industry optimists think that the booming sale of energy-bar brands such as PowerBar, Balance Bar, MET-Rx, Clif Bars, and Luna Bars will eventually match the $2-billion-a-year sales of sport drinks like Gatorade.

What you also may not know is that the PowerBar, the original energy bar, is not the "sure thing" invention of some high-tech nutrition laboratory belonging to Amalgamated Gigantic Foods, but it was the resulting concoction formulated in the small Berkeley kitchen of Brian Maxwell, a University of California track coach, and his then girlfriend and now wife, Jennifer Biddulph.

In truth, Brian and Jennifer, both accomplished runners, were looking for an easy-to-digest carbo-boosting food that fellow marathoners could scarf during a race. It took passion, persistence, and hard work, sports fans, not to mention any and all of the couple's worldly savings to get the powerful snack creation up and running. And even though God sure is up there in heaven, it's fair to say they had to do more then pray it into being.

They went around to sporting event after sporting event, talking up their cooked-up energy bars with other athletes, triathloners, cyclists, mountain bikers, soccer players, swimmers, tennis players, weekend warriors—it didn't matter who, not ever did it matter, because they were about spreading the word, talking about the benefits that the little bars offered, giving away samples. And those who heard the word and received the samples told their teammates and their friends, and they in turn told others and the buzz that was seeded grew and grew and soon it was time to move out of the tiny kitchen in Berkeley and that was a good thing you see, because how can you run a $140 million business from a make-do kitchen and still have room to negotiate a buy-out with food giant Nestle International?

We could easily toss in another dozen examples. There's a variable wellspring of successful products, brands, or services that are the result of buzz-marketing moxie. However, the point to this is just to remind you that the true secret to marketing your dream is simply and emphatically (please believe us) this:

You are what it takes.

If there is one thing in this book that is standout important, that is it:

Again—

YOU ARE WHAT IT TAKES!

Let these words cramp your cranium. Fill your headspace with the courage to dedicate yourself to the all-exalted high art of practicing possibility. A Zentrepreneur is a dreamer turned doer. Doing what you love, loving what you do, no person can hide from such a banquet of happiness. Buddha declared, "Your work is to discover your work and then with all your heart give yourself to it."

In other very important words: Behave your way to success.

Create and preserve the image of your choice. Wed being and doing. A Zentrepreneur knows that one of the wondrous secrets to marketing your dream is hidden in your daily routine. With clarity of intent, commit your mind, soul, spirit, talent, intelligence, and passion to your cause and vision. Be the rootstock for the kind of great products and exemplary services that surprise and elate people. Make it your goal to turn everyone of your customers into an evangelist. Be an innovative imagineer of newer, better. Be a creator of cool. A builder of buzz. A mover of myth. A Michelangelo of motion. Act, act, and act! And give them the best stuff you can come up with . . . and become the topic of as many watercooler conversations as you can . . . and send out brochures . . . and post your flyers . . . and send out thank-you cards or gifts to someone who referred you . . . and create promotional offers . . . and give away samples . . . and donate your time, services, or products to fund-raisers or charity . . . and garner goodwill . . . and join professional and social organizations where you will meet people that can help you communicate who you are and initiate grassroots marketing . . . and champion your Website . . . and . . . and. . . .

You do have a Website?

Don't you—

—have a Website?

Helloooo, what color is the sky in your world? How many suns? Down here on this blue marble, the Internet is here. No matter what it is that you offer or do, people look to find out more about you online. Even though the Net is still in its infancy, more than half the population of the United States uses it in their daily lives. And that number is growing with each sunrise. So if you don't have a computer with a modem, get one. If you don't have a Website, get one. Now! Because truth is the truth and quite simply stated: Out of site . . . Out of mind.

Having the greatest product or having the best service is no longer enough in today's competitive and complicated marketplace. You must be technologically savvy. You can't be a not-com; it's crucial that you become a dot-com. Get your Web feet wet. Realize that having your own Website allows you to powerfully promote your presence, post and disseminate information about your company twenty-four hours a day. But better than that, your Website can be the door opener that begins your relationship with the customer. Electronic shmoozing rules! Use your Website as a powerful tool to rouse, build, and enhance buzz. Cultivate testimonials. Elevate endorsements. Have a tell-a-friend button that allows users to forward a message about your products or services. Buzz from friends and colleagues carries a lot more weight than assertions from a marketing department. Tell-a-friend is the raucous roar of people talking to each other—about you, your business, your product, or services. Offer a query section, message board, or chat room that will become a fulcrum for connecting, stimulating conversation and customer-to-customer exchanges that also facilitates word of mouth. Take advantage of the proliferation of Internet newsgroups, chat communities, and discussion forums that can draw the attention of potential users. When word of mouth becomes *word of mouse*, you can, like lightning, accelerate buzz across town, across countries, across continents. Stimulating the spread of buzz can propel the slightest comment into a full-blown dialogue of discovery for the interested multitudes. That's what the Web is all about. Understand that the Internet is not only a medium of communication; it's also a medium of community, too. A vehicle that encourages socializing and the sharing of information that leads us out of the darkness. It is quite a spectacular thing to comprehend. And it still knocks me out.

In the end, for all the hubris, buzz is simply a trail of breadcrumbs for fresh eyes and ears to follow. A highly charged energy that can help lead the way to an awareness of something that might not have been. Let's face it—this book is as good an example of buzz as any, since in all probability it was some genus of buzz that has brought us together. It certainly was buzz that inevitably sparked Ron and me to get up and get out these pages finally filled and delivered—

On time.

Looking back, I remember the hinge moment so clearly. It started when we received a polite e-mail from an inquisitive young lady, a fellow Zentrepreneur who had launched her own tech-support company in Portland. The reason for her contacting us was to ask how soon she would be able to put her eager little hands on our newest bound creation. And yes, my writer's heart was pleased at her excited interest and anticipation, but it was going to be a while yet because, I explained, our attention had been pulled elsewhere. However, if all stays somewhat on schedule, things going good, it should be—could be—maybe—possibly published in the spring and thank you.

And then what she wrote next really rocked us. Rocked being the right word because she began spouting some of what she liked about the goodies Ron and I already had lurking throughout the spine of the book. In other words, she came armed with material we've laid down—but how could she know? She had to be some kind of mystic. Don't you see, there was no way she could possibly on earth have such a handle on the shapings of what were still to us just chunks, the rough jottings of a running draft. Now what you must know is that there is a certain emotional lunacy to asking a complete stranger how she managed to apprehend so dead-solid much of something that was still set aside sacred, not yet spit-shined for viewing.

"I picked up some buzz about it on the Internet," she boasted. "Go see for yourself."

Which I did.

And I was stunned.

YUANJIAN

Foresight

Chapter Seven
FORESIGHT

AN EYE FOR AN I—
MAKE YOUR VISION
YOUR MISSION

A dragon achieves its destiny

by creating it.

We want to impart to you now a most genuinely dazzling notion, one that will not be illumined in any of the business classes in America's hallowed Ivy League deities, and here it is in a paragraph all its own:

The meaning is in the dreaming.

Each day that dawns, recognize that a dream is a powerful nexus that attaches the mind to the soul, allowing you to create your personal purpose, your vision for what is truly important to you. More than that, by empowering your creative imagination, you cross over the shadow threshold to future possibilities. Vision energizes your enthusiasm, confidence, passion, persistence, and beliefs. Vision reaches beyond what is into an exhilarating world of what can be. It is the life of an idea. And it is this energy of conception swirling all around that gets us helpless with happiness and at the same time most haunts our dreams. I hope we understand this by now, that there are endless ideas waiting to be born. It is the Zentrepreneur that allows their birth.

Again: *While entrepreneurs get hold of an idea, Zentrepreneurs let an idea get hold of them.*

And allows the inexplicable energy of the idea to grab and sweep them off their feet. Drawn by the excitement and potential of the idea, one becomes aware of the frenetic forces at play, yielding to the gestation of possibilities that creates the course for success. And lets us move always and forever onward.

While there are many formulas for grappling with the task of marketing an idea, the upside-down wisdom is that the beginning of business demands the creation of a written mission statement. Half true. While the terms mission statement and vision statement are often interchanged one for the other, a vision statement is a mental magnet that pulls you naturally in the direction of your life purpose. The word vision, from the ancient Sanskrit *vijnana*, means higher wisdom. It is higher wisdom that is in all ways pregnant with possibilities, and provides the fertility and then the fusion and ultimately the invariable birth and growth of an idea. Listening to what's truly inside, a Zentrepreneur allows the idea to take over. Yielding to the confluence of innovation, a new way of seeing and a new way of being are advanced. Visioning the different, the Zentrepreneur discovers the different.

While the entrepreneur pretends to know what's next, a Zentrepreneur imagines what's next.

And believes in it deeply.

A mission statement flows directly from the vision—it is the implementation of the inspiration, which captures the essence of the dream and treats all to the almost mystical insight. A great mission statement tells the world who you are, why you are here, what it is you are going to do. Bestselling author Tom Peters, a very bright man and one of this country's most successful business gurus, calls for your mission statement to be a vehicle that puts your passion out in the open. He is, of course, only absolutely right. Put your dream out there. Your heart and soul too. A mission statement should be a very strong motivational statement that drives your business, attracts customers, and brands your products. What kind of glorious difference do you want to make in the world? What is it about your mission that is wildly persuasive and sufficiently distinguishes you from your competitors? Is it easily understood and action-ready? Is it committed to the excellence demanded by the market-place? Does it deliver the values and benefits you want to express? Will it elicit an emotional, motivational response? Does it deliver on your commitment to do, to be?

Break out your Mac or crack open a box of Crayolas and start writing a mission statement that will propel and put the world on notice. One that is programmed to over come the parlous slippery slope of success and allows you to face any oncoming avalanche of challenges. One that shows us what you're made of. Long, short, a paragraph, a sentence, doesn't matter. When you have it down, do yourself and the rest of us that are part of your world a favor . . .

Read it. . . .

Feel it. . . .

Believe it. . . .

Then most of all . . . do it!

And share it. With everyone. Don't keep it buried in a paperwork dungeon with your startup papers. Keep your mission statement in front of as many eyes that can see. Get comfortable having it around. Post it on the wall, bold-print it at the front of your employee manual. Make it a mind-share manifesto. To be effective, your business must extol its goals and aspirations on a daily bases. Do you have employees? If you do, as a regular exercise, ask them to relate your company's mission. The answer, or lack of one, will shock and sadden. Those that are on your team should never lose sight of why the business was started and what it is that you hope to accomplish. The success of any business is no more or less than the collective will of the people involved. You can shape that will. It is imperative that each and everyone be an activist, a co-conspirator in going after the greatness that is out there. A revolution is what we are talking about here. An infectious call to arms. Making a movement within, creating an infectious virus of verve that spreads outside. Start an insurrection. Be a heretic—heretics start revolutions. Get people to defect to your cause. See the difference, be the difference that can draw others. For the mission statement to hit its mark, the connectives between the vision and mission must be there, to give a sense of uplift, to ennoble, direct, and guide. The ancient masters declared, if you do not know the destiny you seek, it will not matter which path you take. Indeed.

Okay, readers, want an example of a mission statement? Here's one that the aforementioned Tom Peters has used as a model in his across-the-country, standing-room-only seminars.

Alas, it's also a very near and dear one.

As Ministers of The Republic of Tea, our not-so-covert mission is to carry out a Tea Revolution. Our free and open immigration policies welcome all who wish to flee the tyranny of coffee-crazed lives and escape the frazzled, fast-paced, race-to-stay-in-one-place existence that it fuels. In our tiny land, we have come to learn that coffee is about speeding up and losing sight, while tea is about slowing down and taking a look. Because tea is not just a beverage, it is a consciousness-altering substance that allows for a way of getting in touch with and taking pleasure from the beauty and the wonder life has to offer. We will continue to purposely canvas the globe and will not rest until we see these teas steaming in the cups of men, women, and children everywhere, bringing joy and contentment through the sip-by-sip life—a life of health, balance, and well-being.

All right, class, what do you think? Too long? It is and it isn't. Again, it doesn't matter if a mission statement is put out as an easy-to-remember one-liner, a phrase, or a paragraph or two. It just needs to achieve the function of creating notice, setting values, and allowing behavior to support the implementation of the ultimate goal. A great mission statement should begin with a purpose statement that communicates the essence of the vision, the founding purpose, what it is you would like to accomplish. It should have a declaration of change in the status quo, one that identifies the problem or condition to be changed. How are you going to make things different? Pronounce a focus on outcomes and results, rather than the methodology. Again, long, short, doesn't matter how much ink on paper is used. So do not be intimidated. A mission statement need not be a lengthy tome or intellectual discourse, so don't go wondering. To succeed it needs only to hit the high spots, focusing energy, articulating, and communicating the essential quality and guiding intention of your business. Okay, here we go again. The statement that Ron and I keep pasted in our daily planner and live with every day:

"Our Mission is to be the leading purveyor of fine teas and herbs in the world—respected for our unsurpassed quality, unequaled product selection, service, creativity, and presentation."

Short enough?

Here's another statement, without an ounce of fat and says a great deal:

"The mission of Southwest Airlines is dedication to the highest quality of Customer Service delivered with a sense of warmth, friendliness, individual pride and Company Spirit."

Here's one for you that's as good as the game:

"We help people trade practically anything on earth."
—eBay

And our hats off favorite:

"To make people happy."—Walt Disney.

Hear, hear.

Now comes your turn. Get ready for some sublime skull-scratching, spending time, a great deal of time, in contemplative sacred thought, crystallizing your personal statement of resolve. With full purposefulness, honor yourself with this centered, clarifying task. Subscribe to the Japanese concept of *kokoro ire*, the putting in of your heart, spirit, and mind—your whole marrow into the preparation. Like the ceremonial tea ceremony, where the simple act of serving and taking tea is not just the aesthetic act that takes place in the tea room, but a focused, centered act of artistry toward all of one's existence, your vision is the applied art of your being. Do not look at your vision as something out there at a great distance; by purposefully taking the distance out of existence, your vision becomes your mission. As a Zentrepreneur, use your awakened mind to give form to your vision, listening to the echo of your life's destiny. Look inward to move outward on your journey of greatness. This is not an academic exercise, but a living dynamic affirmation of you.

Conceive—Believe—Achieve.

Begin by making the mystical marriage between your vision and your mission, creating your own strong, spirited statement of determination—your preferred future. Get settled in your footing and be clear as to exactly what you stand for, what you want to be, do, and accomplish. Next, more light forthcoming with a shined focus on the lasting difference and attributes of your business, service, idea, or product, never losing sight on what tomorrow can bring. If the connective kernels of your vision-mission statement gel with energy, vitality, passion, and intelligence, then you will have created the most crucial steering mechanism for marketing your dream. So, please, do us a favor here, put the book down and think about what it will take to make your vision your mission. Take a breather, using the time now in order to give this all some good and great thought while it still plays fresh in your mind. Just make sure that whatever it is that circles and lands moves you. Truly. That's all we're asking. That, and just one more thing only:

That it makes you care.

And in a world that has been so brutally dented recently, caring is one of the things that we all should be caring more about.

ZHISHI
Knowledge

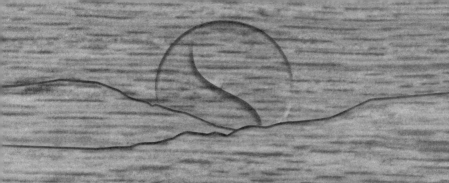

Chapter Eight
KNOWLEDGE

DAYSTAR—
LIGHT THE LIGHT

The brilliance of a dragon is second

only to the stars in heaven.

Never let go the wonder.

Nor the want, nor the understanding of the again-and-again realization that knowledge is the oxygen of success. In a marketplace encumbranced with challenges and obstacles, knowledge is the animating breath that brings the cosmos closer and allows you to grasp the possibilities and promise that awaits.

Nothing matters more.

The masters taught their warrior students that those who were not born dragons can become dragons through true transformation. Remember that, good people. One of the absolutely indelible lessons that can be learned from any successful enterprise is the compelling emphasis that is placed on continual transformation through the perpetuation of knowledge, skills, talent, and resourcefulness. Grow with know or be blinded by the light of another's brightness.

Rewinding back, here are a few examples.

Got a cell phone? Everyone has a cell phone (ugh!). If you owned one a few years ago it was more than likely a Motorola. They were the undisputed numero uno world leader. Their knowledge was analog technology. Back to our question—Got a cell phone? If you do, what kind is it? Think a second. Okay class, all together now . . .

Nokia.

Riiiight. While the folks at Motorola were thinking that they were as smart as anybody, Nokia, a small, rubber-boot company was learning about the wonder of digital wireless technology. Back then, Motorola thought they knew it all. What they know now for sure is that most of the cell-gabbing world today gabs it up on a digital wireless Nokia.

Some make it happen. Some watch it happen. And some enter oblivion wondering what happened.

The business street is littered with sure-shot ruins, unshakable believers who were genuine in their belief that dream-come-true success was made up of achievement and attainment and not an ongoing learning experience. And that's a damn shame. Ask Apple's Steve Jobs who failed to see the wisdom in licensing the Macintosh operating system to other companies. Dig up the bulletproof wizards at Kmart who thought they knew it all only to discover themselves, too late, staggering, trapped topsy-turvy, pushed by Wal-Mart. Then straight off a cliff.

Because it's murderous out there.

You cannot stand on a pat hand. You must constantly throw in your cards and deal yourself fresh aces to stay ahead of your competition. Your fine-honed ability determines both your adaptability and capability to react and respond to the day-by-day uncertainties and demands of a world full of change and challenge. To be willing, conscientious, and hard-working is no longer enough. Neglecting the all important need to possess an expanding accumulation of knowledge is a self-inflicted paralysis that will give over to debacle and failure, and the marketplace offers enough of that up without our help.

Building success requires more than a strong belief in your dream—it requires an even stronger belief in yourself. A belief that empowering yourself with the glories of continuing clarity and distilled knowledge is the surest path to ongoing solvency and competitive superiority. Each piece of knowledge leads to the next. Profound insights come out of newly discovered facts. In order to successfully self-market your dream you must continue to foster your self-expansion. It is the Zentrepreneur's responsibility to nurture not only the growth of the business but also the self. Cultivate your talent, sharpen your skills, accumulate more and more knowledge, never hesitating to pile on the smarts some more. We promise you, and please believe us, wisdom is a weight that is carried easily.

The Chinese have a saying, "May we live in interesting times." Alas. In all of human history, business has never been as rapidly ever-changing as now. As the blather of the dot-gone experience showed us, even with millions to fund your business, your great idea may become stillborn or die a young death without the knowledgeable know-all that today's marketplace of breakaway products and services demands. Lack of experience, not capital, accounts for nearly 90 percent of all business failures. To excel and succeed you must continually learn, search, discover, and update knowledge and skills that will enable you to forge ahead and do battle with the unknown. The ancients were fond of saying that if you know that you do not know everything, then you know everything you need to know. Whether you are new to business or a grizzled seasoned veteran, it is essential that you do all you can to know what you know and know what you don't know, knowing all and every bit of it, is not enough.

And there lies the problem.

Because those that understand this are ruby-rare. Too often, too many are certain that they possess all the tools necessary to build their dreams, failing to avail themselves of the acceleration that the treasures of ongoing knowledge can bring. Expanding your knowledge, marshaling wisdom and ability will help you see past the clutter and confusion that may confine or drain you, limiting your success. Look—Zentrepreneurs are made, not born. The one realization that all Zentrepreneurs share is an intense desire to know more, to respect the long-term need to become better tomorrow than they are today. The *I Ching* extols the view that the secret to successful action lies in duration. Embrace an eagerness for continuous personal growth. Have the humility and the humble heart necessary to identify the knowledge and skills you are lacking in order to ceaselessly market your dream with confidence and competence. Pleeease recognize that this is a good and practical must-do, long-term strategy, critical for the complexities of owning and running a successful business, remembering that many successful businesses may not be well known, but they are well owned.

Forget making yourself president or CEO, instead anoint yourself CLO—*Chief Learning Officer*. Become the glorious and gifted leader of ME, Inc. Recognize that the next best thing to having knowledge is knowing where and how to find it. Subscribe to business magazines and e-mail newsletters. . . . Get your mitts on industry journals. . . . Visit trade shows. . . . Listen to audiotapes while you're street sailing. . . . Talk to others who are in the same or similar business. . . . Learn from their experiences. . . . Attend classes, seminars, and conferences that can teach you computer skills, marketing ideas, and other occupational acumen. . . . Join trade or industry associations. . . . Navigate the Net for fact-finding information. . . . Investigate effective strategies and success principles. . . . Study the mechanics of business management. . . .

And read, read, read the bookshelves through.

This is not brute work, and it is something that Ron and I so strongly urge you to do. Assign yourself one new book each and every week. Choose subjects and authors that can help you manifest your mentality and feed your Zentrepreneurial spirit. Equip yourself with attitudes, attributes, and skills. Uncover wisdom. Develop direction. Become a connoisseur of capability. A catalyst for change. Enable yourself to take the dares. Marketing success is an act of exploration. A commitment to a quest to be the kind of best that can deliver you to the roof of the world.

Now you may be thinking that with all that you have going on that you can't make time for this sort of thing. Understand that while you can't someone else is. Your competitors perhaps. Competitors who all walk a similar earth but with a realized discipline that books are a lifeblood that can change their lives.

And destroy your power in the marketplace.

Zentrepreneurs' success is the result of exerting their will to transform themselves, grow and evolve, knowing that they can help change the world as it is into the world it can be. But humility must lead the way. Albert Einstein who was only smarter then all of us stated, "The more I learn, the more I realize I don't know." You must dive deeply into the mastery process. Marketing your dream is, above all else, a state of mind. Wisdom not capital is the quintessential currency needed to champion your idea. Own up to your weaknesses and deficiencies—your Achilles heel. Then grant yourself the capacity to trap lightning in a bottle. It is of abiding importance that you do all you can to rearrange your molecules to become the rich tapestry of brilliance that can and will rocket you to twinkle with the stars.

Acknowledge knowledge. Please.

Now we never bet against wisdom and we're not going to start now, so what follows is some common business banter we hope you already know. If you don't, you should. Much of this is beginning, bare-bones basics that your competitors certainly already have. At any rate, it's a good way of measuring your personal pool of knowledge while keeping in mind that marketing your dream is not for those seeking shallow waters—it's an adult swim. So take the next few minutes to regard the following FYI pages that can help, enhance, or improve your aptitude. Ron and I have some other stuff to do, so we'll circle back and catch up with you at the beginning of the next chapter.

BUSINESS TYPES.

(Either you're in business or you're not.)

Sole Proprietorship—The easiest and least costly way of beginning a business. Simply stated, a sole proprietorship is a business that you don't create a separate legal entity for. You operate it under your own name, or under a trade name. You will likely pay fees to obtain registering the business name, a fictitious name certificate also called a DBA (Doing Business As), and other necessary licenses. Attorney fees are minimal in comparison to starting other business forms because less preparatory documents are required. The upside of a Sole Proprietorship is that you are the sole owner of your enterprise and can make any of the decisions concerning the business yourself without having to consult others. The financial rewards are yours alone. The downside is the possible negative repercussions that are the result of not being able to draw a line between the financial obligations of your business life and your personal life. If the business fails, creditors can go after your personal assets. As far as the government is concerned, any and all tax liability is on you.

Partnership—Any business that involves two or more people sharing ownership. There are several types of partnerships, but the three most common are general partnerships, limited partnerships, and joint ventures. Like sole proprietorship, no financial distinction between personal and business obligations can be drawn. All management and liability is shared between the partners unless agreed otherwise. It is paramount that when entering into a partnership that a legal partnership agreement be drawn up by an attorney experienced in partnerships to help resolve any possible disputes. These agreements are very complicated and if not drafted properly can cause a lot of problems. The agreement should include the amount of equity invested by each partner, the division of profit or loss, partners' salaries or compensation, restrictions of authority and expenditures, dispute settlement clause, duration of partnership, provisions for changes or dissolving the partnership, and settlements or distribution of assets on dissolution. Legal fees are higher for this type of paperwork than those for a sole proprietorship.

Limited Partnership—More complex than a general partnership, a limited partnership exposes the partners' responsibility to the extent of their investment. The more invested, the more decision-making authority one partner has over another.

Joint Venture—This is a time-based partnership. Two or more partners may be involved for a particular period of time. When the time has expired, the partnership is dissolved.

Corporation—Here's where you get to put the "Inc." after the name of your business. More costly to organize then the above formations, you may incorporate without an attorney but legal and accounting advice really is a must. Becoming incorporated allows you to be a separate entity from your business. This means that the business enters into contracts, pays taxes on its own, and provides the best shielding from personal liability for its owners except where fraud is involved. Control depends on stock ownership, not the number of stockholders. Whoever has the largest block of stock ownership controls the corporation. With 51 percent of the stock, an individual or a group is able to mandate policy decisions. There are two types of corporations, the basic "C" corporation which was just described and the "S" corporation. The difference between the two are the ways in which the businesses are taxed and profits are distributed.

Soul Provider—Someone who endeavors to study and practice, to live a life where the creative spark, the inner illumination of spirit, talent, and uniqueness, is put into motion, fostering growth that not only enriches one's own life, but the lives of others as well. But more than that, someone who has made his or her own life noble and rich beyond counting by simply living a dream defined. The life of a Zentrepreneur.

BUSINESS PLAN

(Failing to plan is planning to fail.)

A business plan is a communicative tool, which conveys your ideas, research, and plans to others. It should list your goals and objectives and the means in which they will be accomplished. Additionally, it includes the business concept, business summary, business description, the environment and opportunity of the market, the relevant competition, industry specific conditions, financial data, assumptions, and projections. A business plan can be any number of pages, depending on what it takes to convey the complete message.

MARKETING PLAN OUTLINE

(If you do not have a written plan, you do not have a plan at all.)

Marketing Overview—A brief description or synopsis of your primary objectives, including the major actions involved to achieve the strategic goals of marketing your service, product, or idea to your targeted market.

Mission Statement—The philosophy of your business. The what and why of your business. Who it is you wish to serve and why it is you want to serve them. A short, stirring description regarding how your business will conduct itself.

Objectives—An overview of the marketing objectives, actions, growth, and sales goals that you will achieve within a specified time period.

Market Definition—A profile breakdown of who or what the market is, identifying the needs of the target market and how your services, products, or idea will meet and satisfy those needs. Define all aspects of the market and include all pertinent demographic information, i.e., the scope of the market, the size, growth potential, and longevity.

Product Definition—A detailed synopsis of your product, service, or idea and its success proposition—why and how it will fill the needs and wants of the market? What void will it fill? How innovative is it? What about it is unique or different? How can what you do or have be clearly distinguished or differentiated from your competitors? What is it that you will do more compelling than your competition? (This is called USP—Unique Selling Proposition.) How will you position what you offer to be received as the reason to be chosen over your competition?

Competitive Analysis—Who are your competitors? How do you compare in price, quality, and service? Define the opportunities that you see. Why do you think that you can compete with them? What are the competitive strengths and weaknesses? What one or two weaknesses will you target to exploit? Discuss your plan to overcome their strengths and your weaknesses.

Strategic Tactical Measurement—A discussion of how you will revisit and evaluate the performance of your plan. A timetable with a pre-defined chronology of when to review your progress, the size of your customer or client base, the state of your fiscal situation. What are your internal strengths and weaknesses? Define each problem or strategic opportunity that exists. A good idea is to review quarterly or even monthly. This will allow you to quantify and measure the success of your plan and permit you to make any adjustments or changes in your overall strategy.

Action Plan—A detailed blueprint describing how you will reach your goals and objectives. What will it take and how will you accomplish it? How long will it take to see a measurable result? Identify the financial and human resources you will need.

Budget—The realistic collective costs required to implement the action plan. What you think is necessary for the business to succeed. Describe how the monies allocated will be used to carry out each aspect of the plan. Include common expense items such as overhead.

TODAY'S LINGO

(A word or two can lead to ten thousand things.)

Address—Where a Website resides out there in cyberspace.

Bookmark—A way to mark and save your favorite or frequently visited spots on the Internet so you can return to them without typing in the Web address.

Browser—The software program that accesses pages and information on the Web. Examples include Microsoft Internet Explorer and Netscape Navigator.

Chat—A program that allows you to talk to someone in real time over the Internet, no matter where their location in the world.

Domain Name—The address or "URL" of a Website. The www.com., .org, .biz, or .edu. Many companies can be found by simply typing in the company name and adding the dot prefix.

Download—Copying data from one computer to another or from an Internet site to your personal computer.

E-mail—Electronic mail containing messages, pictures, or files.

Firewall—A protective gate between an individual or organization's internal network and the Internet.

Hardware—The stuff that you can see and touch that makes up a computer system, i.e., the monitor, keyboard, mouse.

Homepage—The first document or page you see when connecting to the Web server.

HTML—HyperText Markup Language. The standard language used to create Webpages.

HTTP—HyperText Transmission Protocol. The standard language that Web clients and servers use to communicate. The addresses of Webpages usually begin with http://.

ISP—Internet Service Provider. A company that sells access to the Internet, usually for a monthly fee.

Java—A programming language used to create animations, sounds, and other effects for a Webpage.

JPEG—Joint Photographics Experts Group. Used to display photos on the Web.

Modem—Hardware that allows computers to connect to the Internet and communicate with each other over telephone lines.

Plug-ins—Special programs you can download off the Internet that allow you to play audio and video.

Search engines—By typing in key words, these programs help you locate the multitude of Websites and all information available on the Web.

Software—The computer stuff that you can't see, i.e., the codes and instructions that drive the hardware.

URL—Uniform Resource Locator. The Website address is often referred to as the URL.

Webmaster—The administrator responsible for the design or management of a Website.

HELPFUL DESTINATIONS

(freeway exits)

Bizmove.com—www.bizmove.com   A packed resource of information and techniques to guide your business.

Business Nation—www.businessnation.com Helpful advice for starting, growing, and managing a business.

Entrepreneur.com—www.entrepreneur.com Offers information, services, and expert advise for start-up and small businesses to help ensure success.

Entreworld.org—www.entreworld.org   Acknowledged by *Fast Company, Forbes, Inc,* and *USA Today* as a leading online resource for small business.

Garage.com—www.garage.com Simply a great site to help you build a great business.

Marketing Today—www.marketingtoday.com Advice and marketing strategies.

Name Stormers—www.namestormers.com   Free guidance to help you create name ideas for your products and services.

Partners for Small Business Excellence—www.smallbizpartners.com Great source to help start, develop, and grow your business.

Smartbiz.com—www.smartbiz.com Full of how-to resources to help you run your business.

U.S. Patent and Trademark Office—www.uspto.gov General information and search for trademarks and more.

Verio Business Center—www.yourcompany.com Marketing plans, business plans, and planning articles.

Wall Street Journal—www.startup.wsj.com Interactive help and sample business plans for start-ups.

Web Wizards—www.webwizards.com Everything to get your Website started and up on the Internet.

Yahoo! Small Business—http://smallbusiness.yahoo.com Information galore.

Young America's Business Network—www.ybiz.com A network of business information for young entrepreneurs.

COMMON BUSINESS TERMS

(So to speak)

Accounting Period—The period of time—month, quarter, or year, for which a financial statement is produced.

Accounts Payable—What a business owes to its suppliers and other creditors at any given point in time.

Accounts Receivable—The amount due to a business by its customers at any given point in time.

Balance Sheet—A financial statement showing assets and liabilities for a specific time.

Break-even Point—The point when sales equal total operating costs.

Capital Asset—An asset that is purchased for long-term use such as machinery or equipment.

Contract—We know—still, you need to realize that contracts can be complex and if not drafted and executed correctly, may not be binding. Contracts should be reviewed by an attorney.

Depreciation—Decrease in the value of equipment used for business over time and is a tax-deductible expense.

Drop Shipment—A shipment arranged to go from the manufacturer directly to the end user.

Employer Identification Number (EIN)—A number obtained by a business from the IRS by filing an SS-4 form. If you are a sole proprietor, your EIN is your social security number.

Fiscal Year—Any twelve-month period used as an accounting period.

Overhead—Business expenses separate from the particular goods or services produced or rendered, i.e., utilities.

Profit & Loss Statement—A statement of income, expenses, and the resulting net profit or loss.

SHANXING

Do good

Chapter Nine
DOING GOOD

TAKE A STAND—
BE CARE FULL

A true dragon transforms action into right,

and right into duty.

Doing well by doing good.

Unfold any Zentrepreneur list of creeds, and reading over it all, you will see the above wonderful line. To put a neater point on it, you need only to accept the understanding that there is an interconnectedness that permeates the universe. That all of nature and all of life is simply nothing more than continued action. That all action creates change and all change creates action, which in turn creates a further cascade of change, resulting in a universal experience of seamless unity. We exist in relationship with everything and everyone. Nothing, nobody, can succeed independent of everything else. Whatever actions we take, whatever our deeds, conduct, and thoughts, all of it influences our surroundings, our circumstance, our situation, and eventually our future. This is why the Zentrepreneur reflects a crucial awareness that by helping others, we are actually helping ourselves.

Doing well by doing good.

And since marketing your dream takes more than hunch and prayer, what we want to talk about here is how the untapped power of marketing-might can overshadow the resources of a marketing mighty. The constant bombardment for competitive consciousness has never been greater than now. Trying to stand out is no skip into the sunset. No matter how rich the vein of gold, businesses are finding it harder to out-advertise their competitors. But by aligning your business with a social cause, community service, or charitable concern, you can avoid many of the scars of the marketplace, differentiating yourself from the competition by creating an emotional, even spiritual bond that resonates, captures the attention of consumers. And touches a nerve.

As we said before—and please believe us—the key to triumphant success in business is to practice your passion. Ahhh . . . but the key to master genuine success in life is to practice *compassion*. While passion is the primary means to succeed, the tandem truth is that a strong sense of compassion also exists within those who achieve a glorious life. By compassion, what we are referring to is a concern for the well-being of others and to aspire to seek opportunities, initiatives, and actions that will better the human condition.

A recent compelling survey reported that eight out of ten Americans prefer to do business with companies committed to a cause and that two-thirds of consumers report that they would more than likely switch brands, retailers, or services to one that was aligned or associated with a good cause or provided positive contributions to the community and the circumstance and needs of others. The good and great reason is simple:

Because it makes us all feel like better human beings.

And why more businesses don't come out of their hermetically sealed world to associate with a good cause, frankly we don't get it. To forge a mutually beneficial alliance with a cause or charity will do much in a crowded, milquetoast marketplace to help you resonate heightened awareness, win heads and hearts, and perhaps catapult you above your competitors while contributing your time, samples, or donations in a socially responsible way.

Doing well by doing good.

Provide good works, render goodwill. Deliver an experience that makes life better in some small way. Make your business more relevant to those who will decide its fate. Set out and discover what is important to those you court, what issues texture their lives, what threads of concern weave you together. Make their cares, values, and dreams for betterment the shared catalyst for what can be achieved through a new way of doing business. Customers may lack your courage to become a Zentrepreneur, but they yearn to make a difference in the world. Help others to help others. Give ordinary people the opportunity to be involved in extraordinary things. Linking with a charity, cause, or community concern will help you attract new customers, sway loyalty, build long-term profitable relationships and create rave word of mouth plus most important, this:

By helping to change other people's lives, yours will change, too.

Your belief in belonging can create a different kind of world, one that helps the decent who suffer privation. Know that every problem that exists outside of us has its solution inside of us. And remember that a Zentrepreneur sees the wisdom of never holding out on those who are in need of help holding on.

Pledge to practice generosity and grace. By committing to make the world a better place, your unbridled benevolence will both reach and engage and return to your heart and soul many fold. We urge you to abandon the rudimentary and routine, challenge conventional thinking, and be anxious to travel down this revealing and rewarding marketing pathway of compassion and empathy. We're not suggesting that you market your business or product around a social conscience, but what we are suggesting is that you have one. By becoming a powerful vehicle for promoting understanding and awareness of issues dear, by dedicating yourself to the impelling logic of an ongoing exploration of your interconnectedness with all things and all beings, by recognizing your innate relationship to the planet, to society, to customers, to everyone with whom you deal, your business will transcend.

At The Republic of Tea we embody the ancient Chinese philosophy of *Tashun*, the Great Harmony, when people naturally cared about the world and depended on each other for the well-being of the whole. In our little land we hold this harmonious ideal in high reverence, placing extraordinary importance on the shouldering of moral and social responsibility, contributing our time and treasury to many of our citizens concerns. At the core of dedicating ourselves to positive change is our realization that the future depends on our children. We think it's important to ensure that children receive the love, support, and education they need to become confident, successful, and happy adults. Therefore we allocate a portion of the sales of our Panda Berry Tea to support the Sunny Hills Children's Garden and their programs and treatments of abused and neglected children. We donate a portion of the proceeds from the sale of our Global Tea Collection to The Nature Conservancy, a nonprofit organization that understands that we are all custodians of the Earth and must work to protect and preserve the environment.

And it is with a particular pride that we herald the success of our Sip for the Cure Tea that we created for the Susan G. Komen Breast Cancer Foundation, known for their Race for the Cure events and credited as the nation's leading catalyst in the fight to eradicate breast cancer as a life-threatening disease. This tea is a treasure, allowing us to make a difference in the lives of the approximately 194,000 women who are diagnosed annually with breast cancer. In China there is a now popular, frequently heard expression, "Women hold up half of the sky." In our Republic, these words endear, as this marvelous tea has become a haven from harsh reality. With each sip of our Sip for the Cure Tea, you will honor yourself and others knowing that The Republic of Tea donates 75 cents of the sale of each tin directly to the Komen Foundation to help advance research, education, screening, and treatment. And let us tell you that when the checks are signed, it is inspiring, always, and sad, yes—that, too. But it is so moving and so real knowing that we can make a difference in the lives of millions of women and in the lives of those who love them that the hand takes its own time to push the strokes of the pen out of respect for the courage and strength the amount being given helps to provide. Maybe you don't know this, but it is true: Once you allow the heartening energy of goodness to become part of your bottomline, you become more than a marketer of product and service. You become a purveyor of ideals and hope.

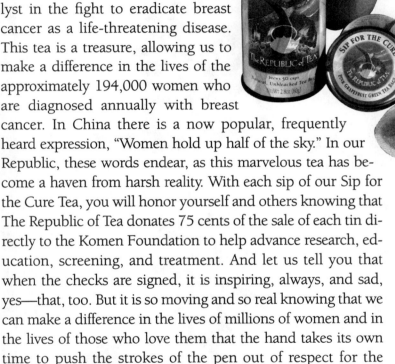

To be sure, in business and in life, a person needs both to survive.

SUIYI

Follow your bliss

Chapter Ten
FOLLOW YOUR BLISS

AN IDEA IS A THING
WITH FEATHERS—
LET FLY

A dragon that does not give its heart wings

will never fly.

Be of no doubt, because wondering if you have the right idea to claim and commit to is an inherent drama that will drive you completely and relentlessly out of your mind.

But only if you're lucky.

While a successful idea may be born of the mind, understand that mounting the courage to create its ultimate existence does not come from the mind. To turn your idea into a visible reality, you must go out of your mind and into your heart. Only by looking into your self, recognizing your potential, and tapping into your qualities of passion and purpose can you actualize all that you will need to set the great idea of your life free, forever directing your destiny. We cannot repeat that too often to anyone who wants to make a living from self-marketing their dream. How your life unfolds, whether your idea succeeds, depends on the choices you make. Choosing to go with your natural expression, following your true calling, will allow you to discover clarity and commitment, the things that give ideas shape and substance and provide you with the gift of harmonious living.

Awaken the way within you, putting the full force of your innate talents, your interests and abilities, all your marvelous gifts into what drives you the most. Diving deeply into your creative being will set in motion that which will release you from the self-imposed bondage of inner fears, doubts, blame, and excuse that prevents you from self-marketing your dream. The ability to create and do, to develop a business by marketing an idea, exists within each and every one of us waiting to be discovered. Follow your inner knowing. Pay attention to inspiration. To listen to the voice of your imagination is to invite grace into your life and provide you with the profound power to journey the path that is right for you. Joseph Campbell, noted philosopher and author said, "Follow your bliss." Gandhi said, "Create and preserve the image of your choice." We say making the decision to do what you love to do can change everything.

Realize that successful ideas are not the end result of some unseen mystical force or stroke of luck, they are successful because they are a projection of what already exists, hidden in the consciousness of desire, waiting to be born, conceived from the heart, planned by the mind, and motivated excitedly by the spirit. Every created thing that surrounds our daily living began at the very first as a fancy of imagination and inspiration. A calling that screams to those that quiet themselves long enough to listen. Pay attention to your intention. Learn to listen to what wants to happen— get completely involved with the inner voice that seeks to be heard. The opportunity that it presents is a path to self-realization. The symbiosis of possibility and purpose awaits to marshal creation. Creation is everything—life is everything. There is no separating the two. Therefore, creation is life and life is creation. The work always at hand is to pursue the opportunity that already exists inside you, removing the obstacles that are keeping it from happening and let fly the great idea for your life.

When you seek your dream, you seek yourself.

What is it that is out there waiting for you? What is it that you delight in thinking about? What is it that quickens your imagination? What is the idea, product, or service that you want to share with the rest of us that can make our lives richer and more enjoyable? Dare to do. Only by opening your heart and your mind will you experience the joy and contentment of being fully alive. Remember again, while entrepreneurs attach themselves to an idea, Zentrepreneurs allow the idea to attach itself to them. And engage the process giving themselves fully over to becoming people who act on delivering the difference, turning the vision of what can be into the view that they see.

A once-upon-a-time beary tale.

Maxine Clark is a friend. She is also a woman who stuffs new life into an old favorite—she makes and sells teddy bears. Lots of them. At age forty-six, fueled by her child-hood passion for teddy bears, Maxine listened to her inner voice and mustered the courage to leave a successful twenty-five-year career in retail to go out in the world to market her own dream. Her idea was to create a place where children could journey to build and dress their own bears. Such a thing. A make-it-yourself bear place, where kids of all ages can select a skin that becomes a bear, choose a digital chip that puts the sounds that they like into the bear, either prerecorded or personalized with a special voice message, then on to the Stuff Me, Stitch Me, Fluff Me, Name Me, and Dress Me bear-making stations, where, after about twenty amazing minutes, a too cute and huggable, one-and-only teddy bear unlike anyone else's on the planet, has been created. First started out of Maxine's home in 1997, Build-A-Bear Workshop now operates over 80 stores in malls across the country and is on track with plans to open 220 more by the year 2007. With sales exceeding $100 million a year, Maxine has been anointed Chief Executive Bear, becoming the largest retailer of teddy bears via the stores, direct mail, Internet (www.buildabear.com), and with offerings on QVC. And, as you might imagine, through a lot of wrenching, exhausting, all-consuming work.

Yes and no.

Pursuing your passion is inexorable—

If you love what you do, you will never work a day in your life.

Ask Jonathan King. He too is a friend who, like Ron and me, has a passion for the specialty food business. Not many years ago, Jonathan pushed his fabulous hand-crafted creations of herbal vinegars, jams, mustards, salsas, pestos, and splendid cooking oils from a card table each Saturday at the Portsmouth, New Hampshire, farmers' market. So sought-after were his home-made glories that he enlisted the assistance of his friend Jim Stott to help him keep up with the ever-growing weekend demand. The thousands of dollars that he took in that first summer were nothing compared to the serious six figure sales that came the following summer. Today King and Stott do over 20 million well-deserved dollars a year, selling their distinct culinary condiments far and wide through their company Stonewall Kitchen, one of the most successful specialty food companies in the nation. You can purchase their award-winning goodies in over 6,000 specialty stores, or from their five free-standing Stonewall Kitchen stores in New Hampshire, Maine, and Massachusetts, and through their mail-order catalog and Website (www.stonewallkitchen.com). Their inexhaustible passion for the possible has given them the confidence to follow their instincts, earning the devotion of discerning gastronomes, as well as something that mere mortals never receive, the recognition and praise from the guru to the gourmand-hostess with the mostest and stock-stirrer, Martha Stewart.

Nice story. How about one more? No biggie, here there are plenty tales to tell.

After all, even bag ladies have dreams.

Take the case of Katherine Brosnahan. Born in Kansas City, her Midwestern drive delivered her to New York, where she landed a job as a temp at *Mademoiselle* magazine, eventually working herself into an editorial position in charge of fashion accessories. At age twenty-nine, she took the time to pay attention to her inner voice and discovered that what she truly wanted to do was to begin her own business. Her boyfriend Andy lovingly offered his 401k savings as start-up capital, and then, even more lovingly, he offered Katherine his last name. Soon thereafter, in 1993, a line of clean-cut, elegant, and whimsical bags were born. Kate and Andy Spade now reign over a $70 million fashion-design company which has expanded into stationery, shoes, eyewear, and now the fragrance and beauty business through a partnership with the Estée Lauder company. Following in the footsteps of Ralph Lauren and Calvin Klein, the now thirtyish Kate Spade is amused at the China-made knockoffs of her bags sold on street corners around the world. As a Zentrepreneur, Katherine Brosnahan crucially realized a long not-so-long time ago how important it is to be yourself—

Knowing an original is always worth more than a copy.

The truth to more heartening come-across is hopefully this: You must not under any circumstance—never, ever—surrender the great idea for your life. Paying attention to your inner voice, developing an attunement and awareness of that particular something that provides you with an intense desire and makes you feel amazingly alive, will open you to the free-flowing force that can create change and fulfill your life's potential. Be alert and sensitive. Within you deeply lies the power that can make the invisible visible and the intangible the real. Use your mind, do not let your mind use you. Summon your instinct. Your creative vision already exists. The transcendent experience is available to all of us. Listen to the innate intelligence within. Whatever it is you wish to be, to do, to have is waiting for you—in need of you. The great idea for your life that is your dream may be dismissed, derided, disparaged, and cruelly ridiculed, but it cannot be taken away unless it is given up on. You can achieve what others may say is unachievable, if you will just embrace your intuition.

And follow your heart.

There are certain absolute truths on this planet and one of them is that the mind can play tricks, but the heart cannot be fooled. The thirteenth-century Sufi poet Rumi said, "Everyone has been made for some particular work and the desire for that work has been put in every heart." While questions, confusion, fear, and doubt are merely mental, the answers for all that is true reside in the purposeful whispers of the heart. Only when your eyes are wide open to this realization will you see the light of choice. Only when you silence the vacillation and confusion of the mind can you hear the voice of your heart. And experience the process through which each one of us comes to discover the conscious contact with our source. Believe in the great idea for your life, knowing that there is an idea for every time and a time for every idea. Ideas are only as unique as the individual that it attaches itself to. While some make the mistake of wasting time and money on the process of positioning an idea in the marketplace, others understand that success comes from the process of positioning themselves.

Understand ideas are opportunities. Nothing more, nothing less. Pregnant with promise, teeming with potential, they are fluid and adaptive, waiting to be brought to fruition, a catalyst for transformation that pulls and urges forward, allowing for the kind of dream delivering we need so much on Earth these days. First and last, they are serendipitous openings for glory and joy, waiting for that certain individual whose unique time it is to deliver it out of the darkness, but for now what we care about is you.

So here's the one final thing we want you to know . . .

It's always your time.

ZIXIU

Prepare yourself

Chapter Eleven
PREPARE YOURSELF

BREAKFAST SERIAL—
SNAP, CRACKLE, AND POP

Without rightful practice,

a dragon cannot exist.

Take care to take care.

There is much to master along the dream-seeking path, but nothing more important than the magnificent mastery of self. For thousands of years long, the dragon has been a symbol of manifestation and transformation. The actualization of the dragon and the Zentrepreneur are one and the same, the grand creation of a purposeful self. As Zentrepreneurs we must wake up all of our days ready to journey through the portal of purpose, choosing to make a life of courage, creativity, determination, and well-being our daily routine. Begin each day with a hearty breakfast bowl full of *this is your day—this is your time*. Empower yourself with get-up-and-go vitality, balance, and spirit. Fortify yourself with a strong physical platform of boundless energy and stamina. In order to awaken the way within and be the committed fearless champion in the cause of your vision, you must make what follows the sum and substance of your everyday. You must take care to take care.

A touchstone here that would be useful to remember is the Japanese *Bushido* or " The Warrior's Way." This system of strict codes that guided the noble samurai is still spoken of with wonder and with good reason. It includes timeless principles that can offer the aspiring Zentrepreneur an ideal standard of serial behavior that emphasizes the kind of steadfast internal daily commitment that will lead you to achieve your objectives and carry over to other aspects of your life. By accomplishing discipline, practicing preparation, possessing strength and the ability to yield, you will importantly hone your wisdom and sharpen your accuracy of action. More importantly, you will be able to overcome adversity, setbacks, and failures. Most importantly still, you will become a master.

Even though the samurai's combative skills were the result of rigorous practice and demanding deftness, it's important for you to know that all training and technique was total, involving the mind as well as the body. This philosophy of "the sword of no sword" was the ultimate *Bushido* conviction. That the greatest mastery was the samurai's aptness to follow both the path of the sword and the brush, achieving genuine harmony between strength and art, the body and mind. By possessing an iron will and indomitable spirit, a sense of purpose and place, the true warrior would not fail in doing anything, overcoming most difficulties without drawing his sword—the sword of no sword.

Marketing your dream, living the life of your deepest desires, can only be attained through such self-mastery—a life of confidence, resolve, and action. Like the *Bushido*, you too must commit yourself fully to manifesting your ability. But understand that wanting to will not be enough. Willing to will not be enough. There is no will or want, there is only to do. You must do in order to master the circumstances of life or risk having the circumstances of life master you. The weight of it bringing you and your cherished dreams down.

No out of the blue notion, research any measure of greatness that you admire, from ideas to people, from successful products to thriving services, and you will clearly come to discover the strategies and principles of self-mastery as the essential cornerstone. The fact is personal and professional achievement is the result of an effortless almost invisible ability to respond and actualize through the integrating of certain habits, a mastering of your inner world that allows you to master the outer world. Indeed, by adopting the exemplar starbursts of the *Bushido* philosophy, we can empower ourselves to make the difference between fulfillment and despair—your becoming one of the few or languishing as one of the too many.

The fundamental foundation for self-mastery is self-discipline. Discipline is the seed of success that will germinate the deep roots to inner-power, the virtue incarnate that permits you to block out those voices that create tremendous tension, insecurity, fear, and doubt and allow yourself a unity of purpose and mind, a focus on listening to the authentic, meaningful dialogue of your own heart. More simply defined, discipline is promise-keeping, dedicating yourself to yourself to uphold the mindful state needed to integrate the habits of achievement into your daily routine.

Do not let others block your light. You must accept responsibility for yourself and the sacrifices for the vision you see. To master discipline is to overcome self-indulgence with an attuned awareness for what it takes to live the essence of self-determination every day. Directing your inner-strength away from the unimportant, directing your energy and focus toward the activities that can make a measurable difference in reaching your goals must be your mantra. Giving up the familiar, comfortable, everyday ways of your living and thinking is but a start. Tapping into your discipline, getting up a little earlier and going to bed a lot later, knowing that it is you who must pump yourself regularly, avoiding the distractions of B-ball on ESPN or a TV show that is your can't-miss favorite, declining an invitation to a get-together lunch with friends are but a minuscule fraction of the sacrifices you will need to make in terms of the self-mastery necessary to stay passionately planned. The needs and wants of a business demand awareness, attention, and importance. A total presence in the here and now. Discipline is the mind-set that guards against the temptations of complacency, mediocrity, self-pity, boredom, and the shirking of responsibility. It is a conscious commitment to engage positive initiatives and behaviors. Discipline is, in itself, a life art. It is an art of accomplishment that will allow you to stay focused and in control, taking the substantive steps to fulfill your highest vision.

A model that may be helpful to make this play is the symbolic sensibility that the Zentrepreneur finds in the poetic postings when strolling the world's most beautiful and inviting gardens. The signs' wording, a flowering of being, a guide rather then a direction, offering clarity and confidence by decreeing, "Stay on the path." Yes, yes, yes! What true tutelage. Adhere to the ecstatic rhythms and metrics of what you aspire to, possessing the core confidence and intent needed to stay the course, face to the front, vigorously nailing your goals in your quest to have success grace you.

Putting a magnifying glass to it, the greatest impediment to success is the self. Use the force of a disciplined mind-set as the catalyst that activates conditions of change. If you haven't the knowledge or the skills to transform, you can devote the energy to acquire them. If you lack the capital to further your idea, you will find a way or begin on a shoestring budget of fettered finance. If you haven't the support of those close to you, you will summon up the self-renewing courage to overcome that obstacle as well. If your dream is big enough, circumstance won't count. The not-so secret here is to empower yourself to power yourself. Accept personal responsibility for expending the energy to take on the essential tasks needed to fulfill your dream that lies in wait. Energy directed from intention precedes and initiates the transformation you desire. Lending yourself easily to the process you will feel the profound surge of forward momentum, experiencing the great power that comes when you align your actions with your purposeful self.

Become adept at practicing preparation. Be broadly based. Marketing your dream successfully demands a lot of heavy lifting—there's more to it than an ability to provide product or service. You must be knowledgeable in the ways of management, accounting, organization, technology, and the myriad of sound business skills, embracing an unrelenting amount of planning and proficiency, all tasks of oneness that will constantly challenge and force you to your learning edges. No matter. A Zentrepreneur's mind is limitless, its potential inexhaustible. And once you understand that the brain cannot hold the mind, you free yourself to turn your dream into a radiant reality, experiencing the greatest exhilaration it is possible to know.

Touching the divine.

But realize please, while taking on the quest of marketing your dream you will never be able to stay home and rest. Solving one problem you will find yourself safe for only a blink because you will always be presented with the havoc of another, the struggle starting again. Know that the ripsaw back-and-forth of plateaus and setbacks, advances and reversals, are an absolute in the daily business experience. Embrace the ebbs and flows as an invitation to develop new patterns of deeper mastery and behavior. Look upon it as an opportunity for you to persevere and transform yourself and those unpredictable circumstances which offer up challenges without regard for your best-laid plans.

When the world becomes too little or too much, endure with persistence. Know that the way to endure is to have the strength to yield, to change course as need be. Mirror yourself in the movement of water. There is no element more yielding than water—it is the softest most yielding thing, yet it is able to overcome the hardest and the strong. Its innate and effortless power is such that it can ultimately change whatever it comes in contact with, wearing away the hardest rocks, or rusting away the strongest steel. Fluid and flexible, water twists and it turns, flowing around, over, under, sideways, down, it changes its direction freely along the way. There is nothing that water cannot overtake, yet its quintessential nature is to yield, to give way. Rivulet or river, water has the relentless power to transform and restructure things that stand in its path. As do you. Know that you too have the depth and capacity to effectively navigate the uninvited tide of obstacles with a mindful spirit of flow, changing jeopardy into opportunity, defeat into victory. Facing problems and challenges with optimism and tempered strength is a powerful tool for transforming them. But in order to do all this and more, you must for each new day, first and foremost, take care to take care.

In other words, wellness matters!

Greatly.

Simply put, the constitution of a Zentrepreneur, is to have one. To keep pace with reality and thrive, to meet the sometimes amazingly complicated and difficult demands of creating a business, marketing an idea, product, or service, requires that you be both physically and mentally resilient and in good health. Your vision of your future must include a conscious pursuit of personal wellness, an intentional decision to adopt a philosophy that embraces and integrates the principles of optimal health, balance, and well-being. In order to function more effectively and have the energy reserves to stay creatively engaged with patience, persistence, and emotional penetration, it is you who must accept the responsibility of self-care. For health is to the body what profits are to a business. Where would one be without the other? If anybody shows you a list of the attributes required to take on the challenges of self-marketing your dream, don't go on to the second item if the first item isn't a vitality of mind, body, and spirit. Your health and wellness will have a far greater impact on your odds for success then your finances, your age, your race, your gender, your intellect, or your luck. Do not ignore the importance of exercise, fitness, good nutrition, illness prevention, stress management, meditation, rest, and an appreciation for your own unique place in the world. Only by recognizing the symmetry of these inner truths can we realize our greatest potential.

And crystallize our dream into reality.

But you have to be braced for the journey.

Distressing, however, is the fact that almost always, sadly, many are not, the adventure of their venture centering on their fiscal fitness, ignoring the absolute importance of their physical fitness.

Believe it, please, your well-being is your greatest asset. Caring for your self is the single most essential necessity in order for you to take on the demands and rigors of self-marketing your dream. While building a business can be exciting, fulfilling, and magical, know that the dark shadow of loneliness will often block out the light of your day. But also know that even though you are feeling terribly disconnected, you will never be truly alone. Anxiety, stress, frustration, fatigue, and daily pressure will be your constant companion. Smoldering demons that will come to call, causing you to second guess yourself, caught between how to get out or how you fit in. And guess what? You must deal with that as your venture progresses on. That ain't never gonna change.

One of the points to keep linked very much in mind is that caring for yourself is the foundation, framework, and form, that gives you the courage and stamina to deal with your doubts and actualize your success. Anything you do to preserve and strengthen your wellness will greatly enhance your chances to persevere over the inescapable malady of daily life. With the gamut of more than enough books and magazines available on overall health and fitness, we need only to take the time here to provide you with this friendly, easy-to-remember homily:

Bust a move.

Nothing reduces stress more than exercise. As part of your weekly work agenda, you must make it a point to schedule some form of active, regular, move-your-body exercise that you would enjoy for thirty minutes at least three times a week. Preferably something that will pull you out of your isolation and bring you into contact with other people. While frequent interchange and contact with others can do wonders for your disposition, exercise reduces the amount of adrenal hormones that your body releases in response to stress and will increase and improve your circulation, respiration, metabolism, and vitality. It will strengthen your immunity, help you build muscle, maintain a healthy weight, and send oxygen-creating dynamism to the brain. And we must emphasize that exercise is as much for your mind as your body. Regular exercise stimulates the delivery of greater amounts of tranquillity endorphins, powerful mood elevating neuro-chemicals in the brain. So exercise needn't be limited to Tae-Bo or weight lifting. The first step to preparing the body to cope with daily stress can be accomplished by simply taking the first step. Followed by another foot in front of the other. When the will gets weak, even a brisk walk will recharge your emotional and spiritual batteries. Embrace a doctrine that any exercise is better than none. And you should be thrilled to know that it is a huge weapon to overcome stress.

There is something you must understand, the frenetic frenzy of self-marketing your dream, the surge of change and adjustments, and all of the roles and responsibilities you must shoulder bring with it a barrage of demands, a bane of strain and stress that can rob you of your energy, your ambition, your health, and your joy. But only if you let it. Again, the *Bushido* offers us a behavior of higher guidance: Do not choose between mind and body, but choose both mind and body.

To reawaken and invigorate your spirit with an intentioned energy to create, to do, to be, take time out for a breather. Literally. Make a daily solemn pledge to allow a few minutes of time and space completely to yourself to focus in on your breathing as a kind of stress-reducing meditation. When done properly, the simple act of awakened breathing increases the levels of oxygen in the brain, decreasing the tensions of stress throughout the body, recharging and re-energizing the spirit. In fact, the word spirit comes from the Latin *spiritus*, which means breath. No wonder that a quick study of most meditation traditions throughout the world reveal the practice of conscious breathing at their center.

It's very important to us that you treat the threat of stress as a serious matter. It is not to be taken lightly or ignored. Do not allow yourself to bear the compression. While some stress is actually good for us, helping to motivate and energize us, providing a healthy pressure that fuels our best creativity and productivity, too much stress can jeopardize your health. There is much research out there that indicates unrelieved stress contributes to many major illnesses such as cardiovascular disease, digestive disease, nervous and mental disorders, cancer, metabolic unbalance, skin conditions, and other numerous ailments. Stress cannot be avoided, and trying to do so will compound it. You must deal directly with stress in order to deal away with it. There is increasing medical evidence that practical, easy-to-learn deep-breathing techniques can instantly ease muscular tension and restore a quick mental calm. By practicing a proper breathing technique, one that develops breathing deep into the abdomen, you will stimulate your central nervous system, dilate your blood vessels, and cause tense muscles to relax. Anxiety will melt away. This method of breathing is the method we are born with but trade away as we get older. In our rush-paced, overdriven world, faster has become the dominant metaphor of our times. We have pushed aside anything that takes time, no matter how logical or necessary. The act of breathing properly included. Gasp. Watch babies breathe and notice how they will automatically fill their entire abdomen and then the chest. The diaphragm contracts while inhaling and expands on the exhale allowing oxygenation to capacitate the lungs and massage the internal organs. This destressing deep-breathing method is referred to in stress management research as the breath of babes.

And if you want to pause here for but a moment to give one such popular practice a try, that is not a bad idea. Begin by exhaling completely through you nose. Place one hand on your chest and the other on your abdomen. Taking a breath through your nose, fill your abdomen with air and next your chest. Sitting upright, keep inhaling until you feel your collar bone begin to rise. Exhale, performing the same process in reverse, feeling your collar bone lower, followed by your chest and abdomen. Pushing out any remaining air, with your abdominal muscles, the exhale should take twice as long as the inhale. If you feel dizzy or lightheaded, go back to normal breathing. If you're okay with it, do this four or five times and notice the stress-clearing difference. There are many deep-breathing techniques and abdominal breathing exercises that offer stress-busting benefits that we encourage you to investigate and put into practice a few minutes a day, as a way of decompressing and allowing you to transform the life energy embodied in the universe into energy of your own. The ancients decreed if you know the way of breathing you have the strength, wisdom, and courage of ten dragons.

Know the way.

Know too that good nutrition is also essential to your capacity to cope with stress. Studies show that under pressure the body exhausts its reservoir of vital nutrients that it uses to deal with stress effectively. Additionally, stress can raise serum cholesterol levels, clogging arteries, increasing the risk of heart disease. If you find that you are often feeling fatigued, anxious, depressed, or stressed out, you should examine your diet for deficiencies in certain nutrients and begin a pro-active habit of taking high-quality vitamin and mineral supplements. For example, B vitamins are critical to maintaining a relaxed nervous system, while a sufficient level of magnesium is important to help muscles relax. Subscribe to a good nutritional diet, one high in complex carbohydrates. This will supply your brain with among other things, a reserve of serotonin, a hormone that relaxes. Also, be convinced that a diet high in fruits and vegetables is the all-important front-line defense in providing disease-preventative, stress-fighting antioxidants, remarkable for blocking cellular damage caused by harmful compounds in the body known as free radicals. Free radicals can be triggered by stress and weaken the immune system, leaving you susceptible to illness, infection, and disease. It's also thought that free radicals accelerate the aging process by speeding up cell breakdown. Awareness transforms. Start by beginning a diet diary, and within days, you will be able to take note of the best and worst of what you put into your body. Correct yourself. Because you will have enough battles waiting for you around every corner, we recommend that you read up on what types of foods are best for combating stress and helping you to protect your most important business asset: you. This is a first and most simple step to understanding the kind of fuel you will need to healthily journey your dream path.

And because it is important for the mind of a Zentrepreneur to float free of mental gravity, here's a short list of gems worthy of polishing that can do much to help you ward off the specter of stress.

Prepare for your day the night before.

Set priorities.

Make wise use of your time.

Don't rely on your memory: write it down in a notebook, scrawl it on a Post-It note, or scratch it into your Palm Pilot.

Make copies of your important papers. Always back up your work.

Revisit your goals, keep them realistic, and continue to develop the will and wisdom needed to achieve them.

Break the work down into manageable steps so you don't feel overwhelmed.

Avoid putting things off until the last minute.

Organize and prioritize, identify self-defeating habits and work patterns. Direct your energy and time on the tasks that offer the greatest return.

Accept the ups and downs of your venture as natural events and use them as welcomed lessons that facilitate self-transcendence and growth.

Strive for excellence and not perfection.

Be determined. Go about your day in a positive, encouraging way. See yourself as a deserving vehicle of achievement.

Know that attention is guided by intention and held steady by will.

Recognize that your power to control your thoughts is the power to re-create your circumstance.

Give real service and value to others.

Realize that the present is the bridge to the future.

Remember daily that self-marketing your dream is not a problem to be solved, but a reality to be lived.

Focus your behavior on activities that nourish, strengthen, and harmonize the whole of your well-being.

Because again, wellness matters.

As does joy. As does serenity and happiness. The unspoken tragedy is that a growing number believe that harmony and gladness exist for them somewhere far beyond the edges of their time-bound world. Not so. Bliss and contentment is there for us if we would only be there for it. While we all live distracted by a world blurred by disturbance, there is nothing that cannot be gotten rid off, no burden that cannot be lifted, no care that cannot be dissolved, by taking the time to experience the life that is in front of us. Awaken yourself. Slow down. Be grateful. And then, oh then, take notice of the marvel, the perfection, the natural serenity, and the true esthetic in every moment and every thing that daily life offers.

While an entrepreneur creates a business, a Zentrepreneur creates a business and a life.

This is the Zentrepreneur's highest mandate. And the absolute golden rule.

Embrace the wonder and the wonderment of daily life. Simply we must, all of us, all the time, absorb the awe of the process. How long has it been since you woke up to witness the scattering splendor of a sunrise or took the time to look up and watch the brilliance of color surrender to a sunset, or drop back a bit to be amazed at what a thing being alone with the moon can be? When was the last time you stood still to give homage to a flower, taking the moment to savor the sermon of its fleeting beauty and scent? Have you ever gone for a walk in the woods to watch how the golden glow of autumn flames the foliage as the year begins to fall away?

The suchness of these things are here for you as you are here for them. Do not take for granted how superb even the smallest pleasure life extends. Alas, we get to settle here for a very short span. None of us gets to take up a permanent residence. And while there are limits to the time we all have to live our lives, there are no limits on how we live our time.

Change the tempo of your life. Be mindful of the moment. For today is above all else, a gift. That's why it's called the present.

Sage statement.

And whose wise words these are to go with, who knows, but somebody after a lot of thought said it, maybe it was us.

Matters not.

What does matter is that you make the heroic choice to practice a life of passion, where what you want to do is one with what you do. Put your creative spark, talent and illumination into motion, fostering the growth that not only enriches one's own life, but the lives of others as well. The Zentrepreneur cultivates and holds dear what is within to what is without. Take the time to make the time to do that which can better your imagination, thoughts, beliefs, faith, hope, body, mind and spirit, for these are your greatest possessions. Have more than a spherical awareness of your world, understanding the sweet joy that all future is perpetually in motion and that you have within you the power of inspired purpose—the force to create, manifest, and deliver, whatever it is you want to accomplish in this world. Never forget that you are part of the vibrant unfolding energy that exists everywhere and through everything. You are a plangent, luminous being whose radiance and energy can create the reality you wish to experience.

Believe fully in the divine magic of your talents and gifts—trust that there is an allotted place in this world for what you want to accomplish. Your ideas and dreams are a necessary thread in the weave of fabric that is the material of the universe. Become fully aware of the many energies within. There are powers always present within you that are larger than your knowing and seeing. Embrace the energy of courage and discipline that surrounds and penetrates your existence, draw on its mysterious harmonizing power, striving to remember that the path to success reveals itself to those who have the profound wisdom to see it.

So as we begin to close up shop, our final hopes and prayers for you are that you will prepare yourself for the glorious days ahead . . . And that you will dedicate yourself to provide a wondrous experience as others have created such experiences for you . . . And that you will at all times fill your grand mind with the tenacity of positive thoughts and bold beliefs . . . And that you will appreciate that nothing external, no adversity, difficulty, or doubt, can have any power over you unless you allow it to . . . And that you are deserving and have the power within to live with passion and intention . . . And that you will value the process and make your best effort . . . And that you will claim your vision and commit yourself to its realization . . . And that you will have confidence in the bounty of your imagination and that you will follow your instincts . . . And that you will have the courage to do the dares and live in the openness of possibility . . . And that you will connect with your higher self and inner master . . . And that you will be certain now and forever that a dragon can fly when you decide that it can . . . And then, finally and most of all, that you will simply and emphatically, please—

Take care to take care. . . .

LÜCHENG

The journey

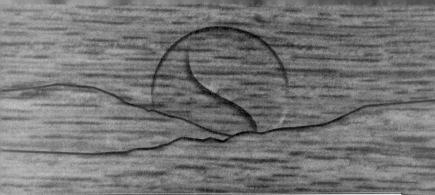

Chapter Twelve
THE JOURNEY

AND SOME FOLLOW A
RAINBOW

A dragon that soars knows that there

is no such thing as a pathless path.

It's all about the journey.

And though Confucius said that a journey of 1,000 miles begins with a single first step, it is our fervent hope that in these pages you have discovered that it is the decision to take the step that matters most—for the conscious path to mastering one's own destiny cannot be taught, it must be taken. Choosing to move yourself with full heart and mind has the ability to move others—indeed it is what spins the galaxies. By allowing your inner dragon to breathe the fire of awareness and transformation, you will not enlarge the self, you will transcend the self, enabling you to see abundant potential and deliver the kind of viable ideas, superior products, and superb services the world is always waiting for. You need only summon your instincts and follow your feelings to take charge, create, and do. Surrender yourself to awareness. That's all it is, this business of self-marketing your dream. That's the great secret. Believing in what's intrinsically special and unique, believing quite rightly in yourself and your ability to play the part. We've been around this block a time or two and after so many years of creating and marketing so many products, we are more convinced than ever that it is you who must become your first customer. That's the true magnificence of any idea. That's the start of everything. Sell yourself first, and all else will follow.

Today we received a wonderful letter from one of the newest graduates of the Wharton School of Business. Not too long ago, Ron and I were invited to address 150 of the school's MBA brighteners, asked to come prattle our thoughts and philosophies about business and about life. It was an enormously meaningful experience, an honor that we will always hold in high regard. But this follow-up note is a treasure. It is the kind of thoughtful jotting that after reading it you could go to bed and snore with happiness, knowing that, thank God, the world would soon be in better hands. This so obviously intelligent and intense woman wanted to announce to us that while others have come and gone, for her, ours was a tremendously valuable visit that had held a light to all possible things—that our words had shattered some of her perceptions, altered a few of her beliefs, and resolved a yearning undefined, instilling within her the wild, barely controllable enthusiasm of a Zentrepreneur. Now anxious with passion, courageous with action, she stated that she will always and forever remain committed to following a rainbow, asking at the end if we could impart any last-minute, furthering guidance as she begins her future. "Yes," we wrote back quickly. And it is a message for everyone, one which we would also like to share here with you, dear readers, before we go:

"While some follow a rainbow, others create one."
And add to that, we'll be waiting for you. Always.

Eyes to the sky . . . .

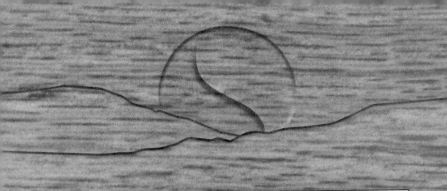

Epilogue

ONE SIMPLE TASK

Thank you for taking the time to read our book. Please share its inspiration and guidance with others, realizing that for every day of living, a book has the power to make such an incalculable difference. More to the point, books can expand your mind and open your eyes to profound concepts and new beginnings that can transform your circumstance. There is so much knowledge to discover, so much wisdom to learn that you simply must read in order to realize your vision for your best life. The person who doesn't read books is no different then the person who can't read them, so please, take the responsibility to visit your local library or your neighborhood bookstore and assign yourself the one simple task of reading a new book each and every week. This is as important an action step as any, as it can endow self-cultivation and provide you with the most single valuable resource for success—other people's experience.

There is an ancient Chinese proverb, "To know the road ahead, ask those coming back." As you continue your exciting journey, it is our wishful hope that for others you meet along the way, the voice you hear answering the questions will be your own.

—Ron Rubin

For starters:

Stand Up for Your Life: Develop the Courage, Confidence, and Character to Fulfill Your Greatest Potential, by Cheryl Richardson

The Republic of Tea: The Story of the Creation of a Business, as Told through the Personal Letters of Its Founders, by Mel Ziegler, Patricia Ziegler, and Bill Rosenzweig

Success at Life: How to Catch and Live Your Dream, by Ron Rubin and Stuart Avery Gold

The Brand You 50: Or Fifty Ways to Transform Yourself from an "Employee" into a Brand that Shouts Distinction, Commitment, and Passion!, by Tom Peters

Survival Is Not Enough: Zooming, Evolution, and the Future of Your Company, by Seth Godin

The Little Engine That Could, by Watty Piper

The Art of Innovation: Lessons in Creativity from Ideo, America's Leading Design Firm, by Tom Kelley with Jonathan Littman

Nuts! Southwest Airlines' Crazy Recipe for Business and Personal Success, by Kevin & Jackie Freiberg

Zen Lessons: The Art of Leadership, by Thomas Cleary

Zen and the Art of Motorcycle Maintenance: An Inquiry into Values, by Robert M. Pirsig

Tao Te Ching: A New English Version, by Stephen Mitchell

Small Time Operator: How to Start Your Own Business, Keep Your Books, Pay Your Taxes, and Stay Out of Trouble, by Bernard B. Kamoroff

Sun Tzu and the Art of Business: Six Strategic Principles for Managers, by Mark R. McNeilly

Winning the Marketing War: A Field Manual for Business Leaders, by Gerald A. Michaelson

The Book of Five Rings for Executives: Musashi's Classic Book of Competitive Tactics, by Donald G. Krause

The Fall of Advertising and the Rise of PR, by Al Ries & Laura Ries

Guerrilla Marketing: Secrets for Making Big Profits from Your Small Business, by Jay Conrad Levinson

How Customers Think: Essential Insights into the Mind of the Market, by Gerald Zaltman

Brand Leadership: The Next Level of the Brand Revolution, by David A. Aaker and Erich Joachimsthaler

Start Your Own Business: The Only Start-Up Book You'll Ever Need, by Rieva Lesonsky and the Staff of *Entrepreneur* Magazine

The Path to Tranquility, by Dalai Lama

Attitude Is Everything: 10 Life-Changing Steps to Turning Attitude into Action, by Keith Harrell

The 100 Simple Secrets of Happy People: What Scientists Have Learned and How You Can Use It, by David Niven

Do What You Are: Discover the Perfect Career for You Through the Secrets of Personality Type—Revised and Updated Edition Featuring E-Careers for the 21st Century, by Paul D. Tieger and Barbara Barron-Tieger

A Good Hard Kick in the Ass: Basic Training for Entrepreneurs, by Rob Adams

Real Power: Business Lessons from the Tao Te Ching, by James R. Autry, Stephen Mitchell

The Tao of Pooh, by Benjamin Hoff

Open Your Mind, Open Your Life: A Book of Eastern Wisdom, by Taro Gold

Emotional Branding: The New Paradigm for Connecting Brands to People, by Marc Gobé

The E-Myth Revisited: Why Most Small Businesses Don't Work and What to Do About It, by Michael E. Gerber

What No One Ever Tells You About Starting Your Own Business: Real Life Start-Up Advice from 101 Successful Entrepreneurs, by Jan Norman

Buzz: Harness the Power of Influence and Create Demand, by Marian Salzman, Ira Matathia, Ann O'Reilly

Feng Shui Principles for Building and Remodeling: Creating a Space That Meets Your Needs and Promotes Well-Being, by Nancilee Wydra and Lenore Weiss Baigelman

The Seven Spiritual Laws of Success: A Practical Guide to the Fulfillment of Your Dreams, by Deepak Chopra

The Monk Who Sold His Ferrari: A Fable About Fulfilling Your Dreams & Reaching Your Destiny, by Robin S. Sharma

Major in Success: Make College Easier, Fire Up Your Dreams, and Get a Very Cool Job, by Patrick Combs

The System: A Story of Intrigue and Market Domination, by Terry Waghorn

Tomorrow Now: Envisioning the Next Fifty Years, by Bruce Sterling

The End of Advertising as We Know It, by Sergio Zyman with Armin Brott

Leadership, by Rudolph W. Giuliani

Bands, Brands & Billions: My Top Ten Rules for Making any Business Plan Go Platinum, by Lou Pearlman with Wes Smith

Sixty Trends in Sixty Minutes, by Sam Hill

Intelligent Selling: The Art & Science of Selling Online, by Ken Burke

The Generosity Factor: Discover the Joy of Giving Your Time, Talent, and Treasure, by Kenneth H. Blanchard and S. Truett Cathy

Life as a Daymaker: How to Change the World by Simply Making Someone's Day, by David Wagner

The MouseDriver Chronicles: The True-Life Adventures of Two First-Time Entrepreneurs, by John Lusk & Kyle Harrison

Eat Mor Chikin: Inspire More People, by S. Truett Cathy

The New Culture of Desire: The Pleasure Imperative Transforming Your Business and Your Life, by Melinda Davis

Bowling Alone: The Collapse and Revival of American Community, by Robert D. Putnam

The Equation: A 5-Step Program for Lifelong Fitness, by Dan Isaacson with Gregory Payne and Mark Laska

Big Brands Big Trouble: Lessons Learned the Hard Way, by Jack Trout

Unique Now . . . or Never: The Brand Is the Company Driver in the New Value Economy, by Jesper Kunde

Being the Shopper: Understanding the Buyer's Choice, by Phil Lempert

Acknowledgments

To Zentrepreneurs around the globe, for their letters and kind urgings asking us to continue the journey.

To Pam, Julie, and Todd, and to Andy, Aaryn, and Shaun, the best decisions we ever made.

To Julian B. Venezky, whose wisened ways we seek everyday.

To our imaginative and teeming-with-talent Minister of Design, Gina Amador.

To our Minister of Propaganda, Heather Innocenti for her flawless diligence.

To our Minister of Commerce, Barbara Graves for her ongoing energy.

To our savvy buzz-maker and Minister of Enlightenment, Debra Amador

To Allan Shiffrin and Kendra Bochner of Image Studio.

A special thanks to Machiko for the calligraphy.

To everyone at Newmarket Press who helped create and deliver, especially the constancy and support of Keith Hollaman, Tom Perry, Shannon Berning, Paul Sugarman, Harry Burton, Heidi Sachner, Mary Anne Cartelli, and Frank DeMaio, and to William Rusin and Dosier Hammond of W.W. Norton & Company.

And, to our publisher mentor, Esther Margolis— when the dig is finally done, they will conclude that she was one of the first Zentrepreneurs.

To all the wonderful Ministers and Ambassadors of
The Republic of Tea:

Alice Johnson
Amanda Dugger
Amy Laxa Caparas
Amy Randazzo
Ann Petersen
Ann Winings-
   Lavelle
Arnie & Judi Gitter
Barb Peterson
Barbara Plummer
Barbara Shomaker
Ben Johnson
Betsy Alexander
Betty Neaville
Bev Williams
Bill & Anne Matz
Bob Sandow
Bob Werner
Brandie Koller
Brenda Streator
Brian Writer
Bruce Trent
Byron Comer
Candace Dagnan
Carol Jablonow
Carol Manella
Caroline
   MacDougall
Cary Combine
Caryle Pastore
Catherine Blackwell
Cathy Sulack
Cece Cotton
Cherie & Ed
   Kimbro
Cheryl Hofer
Christie
   Weddington

Christyne Baxter
Chuck Cohen
Cindy Skemp
Colette Richards
Colleen Kelly
Connie Boone
Connie Kalman
Craig Borgowski
Curtis Crabtree
Curtis Lafaitte
Darleen Schmidt
Darlene Sterns
David Beckman
David Turner
David Welch
Dawn Richards
Deborah Dunavan
Dee Dee Peper
Diane Rice
Dieter Kretchy
Dirk Wollenhaupt
Dollie McKinney
Donna Dirscherl
Donna Newbury
Dori Hettinger
Dorothy Cohen
Edward Blum
Elizabeth Keyser
Erika Mercier
Erol Berkay
Fances Schultz
Frank Nitikman
Gabriella Cross
Gail Germann
Garry Derrick
Gary & Patti Shaffer
Gary Katz
Gary Mascioletti

Geary Ferguson
George O'Neil
George Phillips
Gina Bonnelly
Glenn Guzman
Grant Bagan
Grant McCormack
Gwen Reinarz
Harold Ward
Heidi Cotler
Irv Wynuck
Jack Schreiber
Jackie Robert
Janet DeMeo
Jeff Tillery
Jerry Roucher
Jim DeHart
Jim Gollhofer
Jim Lietz
Jim Weiderhold
Joe A. McGlaughlin
Joe Jakubowicz
Joe Peerlees
Joe Raible
Joelle Guglielmelli
John Casey
John Grob
Judy Roberts-Wabey
Jule Jablonow
Juli Lawrence
June Inman
Karen Uslan
Karen Van Meter
Kari Grabowski
Katherine Carter
Kathleen Finnerty
Kathlene Urbiha
Kathy Azzyer

Kathy Kelly
Kathy Lintz
Kathy Tschoerner
Kelly Holcomb
Kelly Thomas
Keys Allan
Kimberly Mahaffey
Kirsten Omholt
Krissy Hoffman
Kristin Obert
Kristina Richens
Lari DeLapp
Laura Cummings
Laura Lindberg
Lee Katz
Lee Laycob
Leslee Levey
Libby Griffin
Linda Atherton
Linda Champagne
Linda Frantz
Linda Marty
Lisa Onyx
Loree Hanson
Lori Hefner
Lori Polczynski
Lynne Savino
Marcia Shiller
Marco Brinmuhl
Margaret Writer
Maria Green
Marianne Pavon
Marie Reno
Marjorie Brewster
Mark Beilski
Mark Paradiso
Mark Staudacher
Martha Naber
Mary Ann Bathon
Mary Dewein

Mary Mueller
Maureen McAllister
May Lime
Meg Rush
Melanie Coultas
Michael Alter
Michael Dolphus
Michael Jahn
Michele Berg
Michelle Albers
Michelle Foster
Michelle Williams
Mike Patterson
Mike Volmer
Mike Williams
Mimi Carroll-
    Weiderhold
Monica Swinford
Nancy Brikett
Nancy Roucher
Nancy Waterhouse
Nancy Wolf
Nancy Zangara
Naomi Adams
Neal Snydman
Nicole Muller
Norma Eisenhauer
Pam Blumenthal
Pam Gilman-Turner
Pamela Buss
Patti Bowdler
Patty Slocomb
Paul Grabke
Paul Holsombeck
Paula Saatkamp
Ralph Gall
Richard Beach
Robbin McCool
Robert Reiking
Robin Garlich

Rod Harris
Ron Filler
Rose Pierro
Roy Fong
Ruth Graves
Salina Carpenter
Sally Edgerton
Sandra Gaylord
Sara Bauza
Scott Lohmann
Shawn Polhamus
Sissy Hosselton
Skip Simmons
Stacey Jablonski
Stacy Ellis
Stacy Pytlinski
Stan Ferguson
Steve Lohmann
Sue Broeg
Sue Crabtree
Sunny Glassberg
Susan Adams
Susan Titus
Teri Horn
Terri Ritchason
Thomas Dunham
Tina Cowan
Tom Kirchner
Tom Newmark
Tracy Maxedon
Tripp Frohlichstein
Valerie Lamczyk
Vicki Kappus
Vickie Ellerbusch
Vivian Ross
Wanita Statler
Yanina Roca

About the Authors

Ron Rubin bought and took charge of The Republic of Tea in 1994, a two-year-old company that had been founded by the same people who created The Banana Republic. Shortly thereafter, marketing veteran **Stuart Avery Gold** joined Rubin in the company's mission to create a Tea Revolution. In keeping with its whimsical identity as an independent nation, The Republic of Tea calls its employees Ministers, its customers Citizens, and its sales outlets Embassies. Ron Rubin, the "Minister of Tea," is Chairman of the Board. Stuart Avery Gold, the "Minister of Travel," is COO and the company editorial "voice." Ron Rubin resides in Clayton, Missouri, and Stuart Avery Gold lives in Boca Raton, Florida.

The Republic of Tea headquarters are located in Novato, California. *The Republic of Tea* sells the finest teas and herbs in the world to specialty food and select department stores, cafés, and restaurants and through its award-winning mail order catalog and Website: **www.republicoftea.com.**

In 2001, the authors published their first volume, *Success at Life: How to Catch and Live Your Dream*, in the acclaimed Zentrepreneur Guide® series, which now also includes *Dragon Spirit: How to Self-Market Your Dream*, *Wowisms: Words of Wisdom for Dreamers and Doers*, and *Tiger Heart, Tiger Mind: How to Empower Your Dream.*

Zentrepreneur Guide® books are about dreaming and doing, an opportunity to present a path of power that will allow you to create for yourself a success at life that reflects who you truly are. They are about being guided by an inner-wind that can transport you to a place and time where your dreams can and will come true.

Ultimately, it is about the joy-filled destiny you can and must shape for yourself by embracing dreaming and being. That said, it pleases us to invite you to let go of the nightmarish unreality of the reality that has hold of you and give yourself over to the splendor of the dream waiting to have you. It is as simple and as exciting as that.

You will find tantalizing excerpts from some of our other titles on the following pages. Enjoy!

Excerpt from *Wowisms*

YOU must commit yourself fully to manifesting your ability. But understand that wanting to will not be enough. Willing to will not be enough. There is no will or want, there is only to do. You must do in order to master the circumstances of life or risk having the circumstances of life master you.

From *Wowisms: Words of Wisdom for Dreamers and Doers.*
Copyright ©2003 by Ron Rubin and Stuart Avery Gold

Excerpt from *Success at Life*

Albert Einstein, who was only smarter than all of us, said, "You cannot solve a problem with the same consciousness that created it." To underscore, a recent study of Fortune 500 CEO's found that these successful people relied upon set-aside periods in their daily schedules for quiet reflection. The sheer busyness of business requires, demands, this need for a clear space. They reported that some sort of centering meditative exercise was essential for them to reconnect with their intuition and inspiration, allowing them to think clearly and insightfully, helping them to make more effective decisions. Chuang Tzu noted that when people wish to see their reflections, they do not look into running water, they look into still water. By allocating time with themselves *for* themselves, they are able to achieve a personal transcendence that nourishes and exercises mental and spiritual well-being. This effecting of both an outer and an inner fitness has helped them to find the wisdom of the real bottom line:

A healthy mind and body is the true incontestable currency of success.

Now there is a lesson to be learned through this example, actually two. The first is, that one great piece of advice is something we should all be grateful for. And the second: In order to become a success at life and live your dream, understand that you must take care of your gifts.

Pleeease take care of your gifts.

From Chapter Eight: "Secrets of the Temple," *Success at Life: How to Catch and Live Your Dream*. Copyright ©2001 by Ron Rubin and Stuart Avery Gold

Excerpt from *Tiger Heart, Tiger Mind*

Make the time to find the time to create the space for revelation. Relax into receptive stillness, allowing your mind to wander where it will. Research has shown that on average, our minds are busied with some 60,000 thoughts a day. Somehow or other, mute the chatter and clutter that occupies your noodle. If you want to discover and empower your dream you must be willing to take the concentrated action to quiet yourself. The quieter you go, the louder the voice of your heart will become. It is this wondrous voice, your intuition, that is the delicious fruit of solitude. It provides you with your most powerful innate resource, the all-so-great power to silence your doubts, your confusion, your fear of taking control of your own life, as well as the power to overcome the external resistance and frustrations that lie waiting for us all in the dark wood of reality.

Imagine that.

Exactly the point. Imagination is your power to go beyond the known and the unknown to create your utopia. Artist Paul Gaugin stated, "I shut my eyes in order to see." It's lamentable that our focus is always on what exists rather than on what could exist. To that we say, become an imagineer! Pay attention to your imagination, intuition, insight, and inspiration, the flashes that come from out of whatever divine blue, for this is the stuff that dreams are made of.

From Chapter Two: "Dare to Dream, Dream to Dare," *Tiger Heart, Tiger Mind: How to Empower Your Dream.* Copyright ©2004 by Ron Rubin and Stuart Avery Gold

Zentrepreneur Guides®

While some live the life they've been given, Zentrepreneurs live the life they believe in.

Ancient wisdom and timeless philosophies are knotted together with contemporary insights and observations to create Zentrepreneur Guides®, an approach to business and life that helps you find, market, and live your dream.

Zentrepreneur Guides share authors Ron Rubin and Stuart Avery Gold's personal experiences and their philosophy of enlightenment and discovery that has made their company, The Republic of Tea, an enormous twenty-first century success story.

Success at Life
How to Catch and Live Your Dream

If you do what you love,
you will never work a day in your life.

Using personal anecdotes, humor and straightforward advice, the authors show readers how to identify their dreams and turn them into fulfilling careers. "Contains many secrets for living with passion and purpose." —*The New Times*
1-55704-538-0. $12.95. Paperback.
1-55704-476-7. $19.95. Hardcover.

Dragon Spirit
How to Self-Market Your Dream

While entrepreneurs get hold of an idea,
Zentrepreneurs let an idea get hold of them.

With their trademark wit and passion the authors encourage and inspire readers to realize their dreams and offer strategies for success.
1-55704-620-4. $12.95. Paperback.
1-55704-563-1. $19.95. Hardcover.

Tiger Heart, Tiger Mind
How to Empower Your Dream

There is no path to action—
the action is the path.

On this Zentrepreneur pilgrimage of practice and expansion, readers will be inspired to actively take responsibility for their lives and experience their richly deserved dream. "Wise and witty gem that will inspire you to take action." —Cheryl Richardson
1-55704-621-2. $19.95. Hardcover.

Wowisms
Words of Wisdom for Dreamers and Doers

No dream is impossible
if you just dare to live it.

More than 130 quotes from the authors' three Zentrepreneur Guides, illustrated with more than 30 zen drawings. "This gathering of Wowisms—these proverbs of possibility—will ennoble your spirit, initiate your mind, and encourage an awakening that engages you to embrace your fullest essence and unlimited potential." —from the Introduction
1-55704-590-9. $14.00 Hardcover Gift Book.

Newmarket Press books are available from your local bookseller or from Newmarket Press, Special Sales Department, 18 East 48th Street, New York, NY 10017; phone 212-832-3575 or 800-669-3903; fax 212-832-3629; e-mail sales@newmarketpress.com. Prices and availability are subject to change. Catalogs and information on quantity order discounts are available on request.

www.newmarketpress.com   **www.zentrepreneurs.com**

SHARE THE JOURNEY

Tell us your story

As the proud publisher of this book, we hope that you have been inspired to discover the Zentrepreneur in you. The fact that you purchased this book proves that you are open to your limitless potential. If someone gave you this book it proves that someone recognizes your limitless potential. We invite you to share with us your thoughts and experiences about becoming a Zentrepreneur. The best contributors and their stories may even be used in future Zentrepreneur Guides®.

Keep up-to-date

If you'd like to stay abreast of Zentrepreneur Guide publications and activities, join our mailing list (we don't sell or pass on mailing list information). See below for where to send your name and email or address.

All Zentrepreneur Guide correspondence should be sent to

Zentrepreneur Guides
Newmarket Press
18 E. 48th Street
New York, NY 10017

Ron and Stuart can be reached at **www.zentrepreneurs.com**.